Reference Guides in Literature

Ronald Gottesman, *Editor*

W. H. Auden:
A Reference Guide

Martin E. Gingerich

G. K. HALL & CO., 70 LINCOLN STREET, BOSTON, MASS.

Copyright ©1977 by Martin E. Gingerich

Library of Congress Cataloging in Publication Data

Gingerich, Martin E
   W. H. Auden.

   (Reference guides in literature)
   Includes index.
   1. Auden, Wystan Hugh, 1907-1973--Bibliography.
I. Title.
Z8047.55.G55   [PR6001.U4]   016.821'9'12   77-465
ISBN 0-8161-7889-5

This publication is printed on permanent/durable acid-free paper
MANUFACTURED IN THE UNITED STATES OF AMERICA

Contents

Introduction

Critics of W. H. Auden generally ask two questions. They want to know why he revised his previously published poems for each new collection and what his social and religious concerns have to do with his opinions about art. Unlike Yeats, Auden never explained except in rather cursory fashion why he revised or discarded some of his early poems. Yeats worked hard to make all his poems reflect the consistency of mind associated with the genius of a great poet; Auden, in contrast, seems utterly unconcerned about his image as a poet. By their constant and continuing revision both poets cause obvious problems in editing for the anthologist and bothersome problems of meaning for the literary critic; but when revision contributes to consistency or what we call unity, critics will not only praise the poet but also welcome the problems. Whereas critics almost universally concede that Yeats managed to improve his poems and make them part of a consistent world view, many critics hold exactly the opposite opinion of Auden.

Auden never relinquished the right to judge his own poems, and critics consider that an encroachment on their rights. Neither did he ever hold that his poems were inspired or were divine scriptures. Instead, some poems that had become immediately famous he revised or discarded because in retrospect they seemed to him dishonest or plain bad. For his aim was always honesty and good art. It has taken more than twenty years for critics to realize and appreciate what Auden was doing. Only in the last dozen years or so have a few critics decided that it is permissible for Auden to return to his earlier poems and try to make them better.

Although Auden's defenders have grown more numerous than his attackers, few poets of equal fame have received the number of adverse reviews Auden has received late in his career. <u>Thank</u> <u>You</u>, <u>Fog</u>, his last book, provoked the same scornful comments as his early work. Of course, a reviewer has the right to express his opinions—that is what reviews are for; but he is no more noted for humility than other people and indeed is expected by his readers to speak with a confidence that would make anyone else seem an arrogant know-it-all. Perhaps Auden was meant to be the critic's personal gadfly. No sooner does a critic say, Now I have him! I understand what he means! than Auden turns down another path, explores another continent, launches into another universe.

Introduction

Auden has always been just a few moves ahead of his critics, who by the time they have learned how to live with one Auden discover a new one. Maybe he had only taken time to look back, not at them but at himself, where he had been. He looked at old poems and said, "These won't do. I know better now, know more about making poems and more about myself." Even Noah, I suspect, who had his blueprints directly from God, looked at the Ark after forty days of rain and thought that here he could make it tighter, there stronger, and here or there a little more attractive.

The first systematic study of these revisions is Joseph Warren Beach's The Making of the Auden Canon (1957. A1) With Beach, the second question, the relationship of Auden's beliefs, to his opinions about art begins to be associated with the question about revising old poems. He postulates that Auden's conversion to Christianity and probably also his emigration to America were symptomatic of some of the motives behind editing and re-editing the poems. Other critics already in the forties had tried to interpret and evaluate what these two moves meant for Auden's work. Were they a betrayal of his principles in both politics and art? Beach, apparently influenced by these earlier observations, particularly by Randall Jarrell's (1941.B5 and 1945.B5), coupled them with the still earlier assertions in Scrutiny (see, e.g., 1936.B3) that Auden's talent failed to mature. As a consequence, even though he approached his task systematically and rationally, Beach too readily attributed Auden's motives to his new ideology. Later critics then focused on discrepancies in Beach's theory and re-interpreted the data. In fact in the sixties, especially the last half, numerous books, articles, and dissertations appear with essentially the purpose of arguing for consistency, or at least logical development, in Auden, and for almost an obsession with form.

Perhaps it is unfair to assert that in the thirties and forties most writers treated Auden unkindly; at the very beginning he had a very good press from critics who meant well. Nevertheless, they tended to judge him on extra-literary or non-artistic grounds. Those who approved praised only his politics. His adherence to Marxism, for example, was a measure of his worth; leftist critics thought he sacrificed his propaganda to the cause of art, whereas humanists considered him too didactic. Friendly poets like William Empson lauded his techniques; unfriendly ones like Edith Sitwell thought them rather extravagant. If we happen upon an article by an otherwise neutral critic, the chances are good that he is disappointed in Auden because he did not write like T. S. Eliot or because he did write like T. S. Eliot.

Those who want first an overview of the criticism from the thirties and forties before making their own study, will find an objective sampling of these in The Poets and Their Critics, edited by James Reeves (1969.B14), and a subjective survey by William Walsh

INTRODUCTION

in "The Untransfigured Scene" (1971.B11). Afterwards it will be necessary to look at some of the appreciative remarks in the Auden Double Number of New Verse (listed under various authors at 1937.B), the other kind of remarks by reviewers like F. R. Leavis in Scrutiny, Randall Jarrell's analysis of Auden in The Southern Review (1941.B5) and his psychoanalysis in The Partisan Review (1945.B5). Although Auden is not without other defenders, the first full length book-- it is a very short one--appears towards the end of the decade, Francis Scarfe's W. H. Auden (1949.A1).

From that point books and articles appear with increasing frequency; and though they are not all favorable, Auden's champions grow stronger in number and vigor. Probably the best advice is merely to explore the field, but a quick overview again is available in the Reeves book previously mentioned (1969.B14). And every student of Auden must certainly look at The Poetry of W. H. Auden: The Disenchanted Island by Monroe K. Spears (1963.A2), a book later critics consider almost a guidebook to Auden. The annus mirabilus of Auden criticism is 1969 with nine books and dissertations. These and articles in the last half of the sixties and into the seventies begin, at least, to take up what seem to be real critical or scholarly problems and bother less about whether Auden's politics and sex life are consistent with his religious and artistic aims. The trend promises a future of articles with sharper and finer focus on clearer and truer problems, related to his craft and art especially if the present flourishing of dissertations is evidence of interest in Auden.

In collecting this list of secondary sources on Auden I have tried to be thorough, not complete; for I think the task is probably endless. I have relied heavily on the list Edward Mendelson provided for his and Barry C. Bloomfield's W. H. Auden: A Bibliography (1972.A2), now the standard work. I omitted, however, items published in The Explicator since the early ones are already collected in The Explicator Cyclopedia (1966) as well as listed by Mendelson. The later ones require little further annotation than their titles, which may be found in the issues of PMLA's annual bibliographies or the annual review numbers of The Journal of Modern Literature. Mendelson also lists books and articles published in foreign languages, to which I direct those proficient in French, Italian, Polish, Icelandic, and German. I have listed all the English articles from foreign journals I could find; but I beg for help in locating those I have not seen, especially articles published in Asia.

To forestall annoyance in Auden scholars who know a great deal more than I do, I wish to point out a special treatment of the titles of poems in the Index. I am proud of it, of course; but it is meant for students who may just be beginning their study of Auden. Since Auden changed the titles of many of his poems with each new publication, I made it easier to find a specific poem by indexing them under several titles. For example, the poem beginning "Doom is dark

Introduction

and deeper than any sea-dingle" is also indexed under its other
titles, "Chorus," "Something Is Bound to Happen," and "The Wanderer."
In cases where the titles of poems are also titles of books, I tried
most of the time to distinguish the critical articles and books which
treat one and not the other, but paralysis tedious set in after a few
dozen repetitions. I did make, however, a clear distinction in one
case. A critic who analyzes both poems in the book For the Time
Being is listed under the book title. If he has analyzed only "The
Sea and the Mirror" or "For the Time Being," he is listed under the
poem title. The only other confusion of titles I could imagine, I
tried to avoid by using quotation marks for the titles of articles
and no marks for titles of poems. Thus an article using the same
title as the poem it discusses appears in quotation marks in the
Index.

I know it is unmannerly to insert at an appropriate place for
acknowledgments a curse on the thoughtless; but I hope there is a
special hell somewhere for those who steal books from libraries,
slice out articles from journals, and deface print in old volumes.
I could add also those who print misinformation in bibliographies;
but then I may, though I hope not, be including myself.

Grateful acknowledgment is made to Edward Callan, to the English
Department of Western Michigan University for released time during
the winter term (1976), to Lynn Toohey of Waldo Library and the other
members of the Inter-Library Loan staff, and to Genii Greene. Without their help there would have been no book.

Major Works of W. H. Auden

Detailed descriptions of the various editions are in B.C. Bloom-field and Edward Mendelson, W.H. Auden: A Bibliography (1972) and in Edward Callan, "W.H. Auden: Annotated Checklist II," Twentieth Century Literature, 16 (January 1970), 27-56. For Callan's first list see Twentieth Century Literature, 4 (April-July, 1958), 30-50.

POETRY

    About The House
    The Age Of Anxiety
    Another Time
    City Without Walls
    Collected Longer Poems
    The Collected Poetry of W.H. Auden
    Collected Shorter Poems
    The Double Man (New Year Letter)
    Epistle To A Godson
    Homage To Clio
    Journey To A War
    Letters From Iceland
    Letter To Lord Byron
    Nones
    On This Island (Look, Stranger!)
    The Orators
    Poems, 1928
    Poems, 1930
    Poems, 1933 (Poems, 1934)
    Selected Poems
    Selected Poetry of W.H. Auden (W.H. Auden: A Selection By The Author)

    The Shield Of Achilles
    Spain
    Thank You, Fog
    W.H. Auden: Collected Poems
    W.H. Auden: A Selection

Major Works Of W. H. Auden

DRAMATIC WORKS

    The Ascent of F6
    The Bassarids
    The Dance Of Death
    The Dog Beneath The Skin
    Don Giovanni
    Elegy For Young Lovers
    For The Time Being
    The Magic Flute
    On The Frontier
    The Rake's Progress
    The Sea And The Mirror

ESSAYS

    The Dyer's Hand
    The Enchafed Flood
    Forewords And Afterwords
    Secondary Worlds
    Selected Essays

Writings about W. H. Auden, 1931-1976

1931 A BOOKS - NONE

1931 B SHORTER WRITINGS

1   EMPSON, WILLIAM. "A Note on Auden's 'Paid on Both Sides.'"
     Experiment, 7 (Spring), 60-61.
          Analysis of the symbolic and surrealistic levels of
     "Paid on Both Sides." Auden "puts psycho-analysis and sur-
     realism..., all the irrationalist tendencies which are so
     essential a part of the machinery of present-day thought,
     into their proper place; they are made part of the normal
     and rational tragic form...."

2   ZABEL, MORTON DAVIN. "A Dawn in Britain." Poetry, 38 (May),
     101-104.
          Review of Poems. Auden attempts "a reconstruction of
     emotional values, personal and social" and restores the
     "ideals of affection, sympathy, and honor where these have
     become deflated by psychological and sociological re-
     search." The elements of Auden's style "combine to evoke
     a music wholly beyond the reason."

1932 A BOOKS - NONE

1932 B SHORTER WRITINGS

1   GRIGSON, GEOFFREY. "Notes on Contemporary Poetry." Bookman
     (London), 82 (September), 287-89.
          Assessment of Auden as a poet "making a contribution to
     the growth of English poetry." Auden's "greatest virtue--
     the dramatic quality of his verse." Compares and contrasts
     Auden with some of his contemporaries.

*2   SPENDER, STEPHEN. "Five Notes on W.H. Auden's Writing."
     Twentieth Century, 3 (July), 13-15.
          Not seen. Cited in Bloomfield, 1972.A2.

1

1933

1933 A BOOKS - NONE

1933 B SHORTER WRITINGS

1   FLETCHER, JOHN GOULD. "Poet of Courage." Poetry, 42 (May),
     110-13.
          Review of The Orators. In an age of timid poets, Auden
     has courage "to be obscure, unpopular, ...to attempt some
     linkage between the older world of spiritual appeals and
     loyalties...and the new work of inhuman and naked scien-
     tific entities." The Orators satirizes the English public
     school system or is "buffoonery in the Joyce and Wyndham
     Lewis manner" or "fragmentary autobiography" or "a mani-
     festo for an unwritten poem." Auden means to express the
     ambiguity of events, for "there is scarcely a happening
     that does not bear two meanings" for him.

*2   PORTEUS, HUGH GORDON. "W.H. Auden." Twentieth Century, 4
     (February), 14-16.
          Not seen. Cited in Bloomfield, 1972.A2.

3   STONIER, G.W. "New Poets," in Gog Magog. London: J.M. Dent,
     pp. 171-76.
          Treats Auden along with Spender and Day Lewis as a
     group, of which Auden is the leader but Spender the best
     poet. Auden "hints, often with beauty, at a mass of ex-
     perience, of which his poetry is only the iceberg-top; we
     must guess at what is underneath." Reprinted: 1966.B16.

1934 A BOOKS - NONE

1934 B SHORTER WRITINGS

1   BULLOUGH, GEOFFREY. "Metaphysicals and Left-Wingers," in The
     Trend of Modern Poetry. Edinburgh: Oliver & Boyd, pp.
     160-62.
          Declares Auden, Day Lewis, and Spender "propagandist
     left-wingers" but optimistic and vigorous. Auden has "two
     manners, one cerebral and elliptic, the other spontaneous,
     overflowing with humour to the verge of doggerel." Re-
     printed: 1941.B2; 1949.B3.

2   BURGUM, EDWIN BERRY. "Three English Radical Poets." New
     Masses, 12 (3 July), 33-36.
          The "Three" are Spender, Auden, and Day Lewis. They
     have "become despondent over the disorder and lack of
     promise in their lives, and have turned to Communism as a

way out." Discusses The Orators and Paid on Both Sides.
Compares and contrasts Auden with Spender and Day Lewis.
Reprinted: 1935.B1.

3   BURNHAM, JAMES, "W.H. Auden." Nation, 139 (8 August), 164-65.
       Sees Auden as "the most considerable" member of a group
     of communist poets who are "acutely conscious of the prob-
     lem of the relation of their social views to their creative
     writing." Auden has discovered that "he must reintegrate
     his personality" in the light of his social vision. "The
     Orators" signals that "change and reorientation."

4   DAY LEWIS, C. A Hope for Poetry. Oxford: Blackwell, passim.
       A general commentary on the post-war poets. Aims to
     make the reader look at Auden (also Stephen Spender) as a
     true poet. Although the book is about post-war poetry and
     therefore discusses many poets, Auden, along with Spender
     and MacNeice, seems to Day Lewis younger son to the great
     English poets. As such he creates "a necessary link" to
     the past that has been broken by the war. He appeals
     "above all for the creation of a society in which the real
     and living contact between man and man may again become
     possible."

5   EWART, GAVIN. "Audenesque." New Verse, no. 7 (February),pp.
     21-22.
       Review of The Dance of Death, Nothing in the play is as
     good as the opening passage. The verse could "have been
     written... by any writer of dance lyrics."

6   FOXALL, EDGAR. "The Politics of W.H. Auden." Bookman
     (London), 85 (March), 474-75.
       Auden is the "chief propagandist" for the communists.
     He sometimes reduces his satire to a sneer, is "occasion-
     ally hysterical," and at the same time is unquestionably
     sincere. "We may regret his lapses from his own standards
     as an artist, but there are times when courage is as valu-
     able as art...." Auden's "politics invite the disgust of
     the comfortable and the laughter of the secure."

7   LA DRIERE, J. CRAIG. "People We Are Living With." Fleur de
     Lis, 33 (May), 29-35.
       Describes the physical structure and materials of "The
     Orators" as bringing into focus "this country of ours where
     nobody is well." It presents difficulties similar to those
     presented by The Symbolists, who converted "the general
     image into a particular image by mere verbal manipulation"

1934

and "elevated their personal experiences to the position of the universal by a recondite image...."

8   LEAVIS, F.R. "Auden, Bottrall, and Others." Scrutiny, 3 (June), 70-83.
      Auden demonstrates his talent "at its most impressive" in Paid on Both Sides. Leavis stresses Auden's calling it a "charade" and not a "play," for though it has dramatic characteristics, "to attempt actual stage-production would be to misconceive the strength of what is offered." Leavis finds Auden not critical enough of his own work; "the freedom of transition and private association appear altogether too casual" in the poems published with Paid On Both Sides.

9   POWELL, DILYS. "Advance Guard," in Descent from Parnassus. London: Cresset Press, pp. 167-221 (esp. 173-194).
      Auden is one of the poets of the thirties who thinks progress is possible, that "disillusion had been worked out." In "Paid on Both Sides" Auden is "preaching... muscular ethics"; in "The Orators" he moves "towards a militant morality"; and in later poems ("A Communist to Others," "A Happy New Year," "The Dance of Death") he shows "that crisis is at hand." Powell takes up matters of style and discusses in detail parts of the works mentioned. She considers Auden talented but uncertain in direction; "the satiric and the lyric impulses are constantly at war...."

10   SITWELL, EDITH. Aspects of Modern Poetry. London: Duckworth, pp. 238-45.
      A generally negative commentary, giving Auden credit for presenting "the raw material of art" but finding his poems lacking interest. Only occasionally he expresses "a very real and poignant emotion, and the body he chooses for his expression is on these occasions adequate and moving."

11   SPARROW, JOHN. Sense and Poetry. London: Constable, pp. 145-55.
      Sees The Orators influenced by Joyce and Eliot as "an attempt to dislodge sense from the place it has hitherto occupied in writing...." Auden's tone and direct, colloquial speech is "the only single purpose that can be said to run through the book." Auden's "work is a monument to the misguided aims that prevail among contemporary poets...."

12   WARREN, R.P. "Twelve Poets." American Review, 3: 221-27.
      Review of The Orators and Poems. Although Auden has "drawn heavily" on past experimenters of style, he does not

imitate; for he is versatile in style. Some of the obscurity derives from "an excessive obliquity or purely
arbitrary construction" but more often "from an actual
subtlety of thought and effect...."

1935 A   BOOKS - NONE

1935 B   SHORTER WRITINGS

1   BURGUM, EDWIN BERRY. "Three English Radical Poets," in Prole-
       tarian Literature in the United States. Edited by
       Granville Hicks, et. al. New York: International Publish-
       ers, pp. 330-39.
          Reprint of 1934.B2.

2   DARLINGTON, W.A. "A Theorist in the Theatre." Discovery, 16
       (December), 349-51.
          Attempts to refute the premises asserted in Auden's
       "manifesto" printed in the program of "The Dance of Death."
       Auden is either a snob or trying to be noticed; for his
       assertions are false, his reasoning fallacious, and his
       tone arrogant. Takes up Auden's statements point by point
       and responds with artistic and historical examples in dis-
       agreement with Auden's principles.

3   DEUTSCH, BABETTE. This Modern Poetry. New York: Norton, pp.
       241-48.
          A general commentary on Auden, stressing the divergence
       of intention and tone and the necessity for reading all of
       his poems: "His poems are scarcely intelligible until one
       has read them in their entirety." A line in The Orators is
       "the key to Auden's position": "What do you think of
       England, this country of ours where nobody is well?"

4   JENNINGS, HUMPHREY. "Eliot and Auden and Shakespeare." New
       Verse, no. 18 (December), pp. 4-7.
          Where Shakespeare's plays are natural (i.e., not more
       systematic than nature), Auden and Eliot "have oversystem-
       atised their own positions" and have sacrificed "the com-
       plexity of 'real life' positions to the 'theatrical....'"
       Their plays are "manufactured."

5   MAYNARD, THEODORE. "When the Pie Was Opened." Commonweal,
       22 (2 August), 339-41.
          It would not surprise Maynard, after he has examined
       the nature of Auden's (also Day Lewis' and Spender's)

communism, "if all three men ended up as Catholics." He finds them basically religious and influenced by religious poets; and because England had been suffering "a slump in poetry," they had been "received with perhaps more adulation than they deserved."

6   SMITH, A.J.M. "Old Game, New Rules." Poetry, 47 (October), 43-46.
      Review of Poems. Auden's significance is that he has mastered a technique for expressing best "what may be said about the present state of our civilization." Considers some general influences on Auden, some defects of tone, and some comparison with Eliot.

7   SPENDER, STEPHEN. "Airmen, Politics and Psycho-Analysis," in The Destructive Element: A Study of Modern Writers and Belief. London: Jonathan Cape, pp. 251-77.
      "His gift is...of a writer who does not write from rejecting his experiences, nor from strict selection..., but accepting more and more of life and of ideas as he goes on experiencing." His weakness is that he sometimes regards "all the world as ill, so that he expresses a philosophy as soothing as that of a nurse." Spender discusses "Journal of an Airman" at some length.

1936 A BOOKS - NONE

1936 B SHORTER WRITINGS

1   ALLOTT, KENNETH. "Not So Hot." New Verse, no. 19 (February-March), p. 15.
      Review of The Dog Beneath the Skin. Calls it "not a play so much as an imaginative Irish stew." Allot's highest praise is "The verse-speaking was save in one or two instances bearable."

2   EMERSON, DOROTHY. "Poetry Corner." Scholastic, 27 (January 11), 14.
      Auden's work causes adjustments in our notions of what poetry is. Reprints "It Was Easter As I Walked," followed by an interpretation: "Nature moves without decision toward Spring," making the necessity of choice (Man's) seem a "necessary error."

3   LEAVIS, F.R. "Mr. Auden's Talent." Scrutiny, 5 (December), 323-27.

Review of <u>Look, Stranger</u>! and <u>The Ascent of F6</u>. Auden's talent has not matured; he "makes far too much of his poetry out of private neuroses and memories...and far too easy transitions between his private and his public world." <u>The Ascent of F6</u> seems meant for a public school audience and is by and about public school days.

4   LEHMANN, JOHN. "Some Revolutionary Trends in English Poetry: 1930–1935." <u>International Literature</u> (Moscow), 6 (April), 60–83 (esp. 69–74).

Sees the rapid rise of new "Schools" of poets as symptomatic of rapid social and economic changes. Auden is the most interesting of the poets in the group and has influenced the others (Spender and Day Lewis, for example); he has also presented "a remarkable dramatic sense of a collapsing culture, a civilization desperately ill...." The chief contribution "to the development of a revolutionary poetry...has been their <u>awareness</u> of the crisis and the class war...." Predicts that unless the position of British Imperialism changes in the world or that the poets themselves migrate to countries with a hotter class struggle the development of this "intellectual-bourgeois revolt" will be slow.

5   TURNELL, G.M. "Two Notes on Modern English Poetry: I. Hopkins to W.H. Auden." <u>Colosseum</u>, 3 (June), 120–25.

Review of <u>The Faber Book of Modern Verse</u>, edited by Michael Roberts. Auden receives special attention because his poems represent a continuity in English verse on principles the opposite of those set forth by Roberts. Auden emphasizes what Hopkins and Eliot emphasized: "The images suggesting stagnation and decay are not merely technical requirements of the moment, they point to something rooted in the poet's outlook."

1937 A BOOKS – NONE

1937 B SHORTER WRITINGS

1   ALLOT, KENNETH. "Auden in the Theatre." <u>New Verse</u>, nos. 26–27 (November), pp. 17–21.

Does not think Auden's dramatic pieces are good plays but are exciting and interesting. <u>The Dog Beneath The Skin</u> is better entertainment, but <u>The Ascent of F6</u> is the better play because "the conflict is kept steadily in view...."

1937

2 ANON. "Sixteen Comments on Auden." <u>New Verse</u>, nos. 26-27 (November), 23-30.

    Mostly appreciative comments by Edwin Muir, George Barker, Frederic Prokosch, David Gascoyne, Dylan Thomas, Berthold Viertel, C. Day Lewis, Allen Tate, Bernard Spencer, Charles Madge, Herbert Read, Ezra Pound, John Masefield, Graham Greene, Sir Hugh Walpole, and W.J. Turner. They range from a sentence to two or three paragraphs.

3 CLOSE, H.M. "The Development of Auden's Poetry." <u>Cambridge Review</u>, 58 (9 June), 478-79.

    Auden's newly won recognition and popularity serve "to spoil and debase his talent." Such criticism from critics like F.R. Leavis, for example, is too harsh; for Auden in <u>Look, Stranger</u>! and <u>The Ascent of F6</u> displays maturing talent. He has an assured, consistent tone and blends irony with lyricism, and practices economy of expression. In spite of faults in these two books ("a gross lack of care"), they show "a real development in their author's seriousness and capacity."

4 GLICKSBERG, CHARLES I. "Poetry and Marxism: Three English Poets Take Their Stand." <u>University of Toledo Quarterly</u>, 6 (April), 309-25.

    Marxism views the role of the poet as that of educating readers "in a certain direction" and developing "their class-consciousness." Auden along with Day Lewis and Spender refuses to accept this dogma; Auden asserts that poetry must be "an organic part of life" and reflect the infinite variety of life. These three poets serve both criticism and poetry by announcing, in spite of their Marxist sympathies, that exhortation to Marxism or "coercive propaganda" hinders the "communicative process."

5 GREGORY, HORACE. "The Liberal Critics and W.H. Auden." <u>New Masses</u>, 23 (20 April), 25-27.

    Replies to some negative criticism by reviewers of Auden's <u>Ascent of F6</u> and <u>On This Island</u> and lists poets like Housman, Lawrence, Eliot and Hopkins as well as prose fiction writers who have influenced Auden. Discusses the influence of "the memory of D.H. Lawrence" in some detail and declares that some poems in <u>On This Island</u> ("a half dozen") will convince readers that "poetry has not lost its power to perceive the realities of the time in which we live."

6 GRIGSON, GEOFFREY. "Auden As a Monster." <u>New Verse</u>, nos. 26-27 (November), pp. 13-17.

Auden's monstrosity is that he "does not fit...is no gentleman"; does not follow the rules, etc. Generally an appreciation of Auden as "entirely and successfully a poet."

7   HUMPHREYS, A.R. "The Ascent of F6." Cambridge Review, 58 (30 April), 353-55.
Difficulties in Auden's plays rise from their obscurities, not from their complexities. Lists elements of The Ascent of F6 that confuse the reader or spectator: Large borrowings from Eliot in the complication, psychological preoccupations mixed with glib satire, hints of "sickening evil" never substantiated later, superimposition of a symbolic spiritual adventure on a physical adventure, surrealistic presentation of hysteria, three different conclusions (book, Mercury Theatre performance, and Arts Theatre performance) apparently considered interchangeable, and symbols shifting in meaning.

8   ISHERWOOD, CHRISTOPHER. "Some Notes on Auden's Poetry." New Verse, nos. 26-27 (November), pp. 4-9.
An appreciation. We should remember that Auden is (1) a scientist, "a schoolboy scientist," (2) a musician and a ritualist, and (3) a Scandinavian. On Auden's obscurity, Isherwood says: "If I liked one line, he would keep it and work it into a new poem. In this way, whole poems were... simply anthologies of my favorite lines, entirely regardless of grammar or sense." Reprinted: 1964.A4.

9   MacNEICE, LOUIS. "Letter to W.H. Auden." New Verse, nos. 26-27 (November), pp. 11-13.
Addresses Auden's practices and ideas in the form of a personal letter: You do this; I feel this way about it, etc. "...what I admire in you is your unflagging curiosity about people and events."

10   RICKWORD, EDGELL. "Auden and Politics." New Verse, nos. 26-27 (November), pp. 21-22.
Finds Auden leaving social concerns for personal concerns. "The lyric grace of Auden's later poems is achieved at the expense of that sensuous consciousness of social change which made his early poems such exciting discoveries."

11   SPENDER, STEPHEN. "Oxford to Communism." New Verse, nos. 26-27 (November), pp. 9-10.
Reminiscence of Auden's last year at Oxford and comments on the "psychological" process of Auden's embrace of communism.

1937

12   TODD, RUTHVEN. "Writings by W.H. Auden (1929-1937)." New
     Verse, nos. 26-27 (November), pp. 32-46.
          "This check list is for readers, not for bibliographers
     or collectors," says Todd. Includes a facsimile of the
     manuscript of Auden's poem, "The fruit in which your parents
     hid you, boy," first published in New Verse, no. 4 (1933),
     p. 8. Lists all the early works into 1937.

13   TRAVERSI, D.A. "Marxism and English Poetry." Arena, 1
     (October-December), 199-211 (esp. pp. 205 ff.).
          The promise displayed in Auden's early works is never
     fulfilled in the later because Marxist doctrine fails "to
     add strength and maturity to his natural gifts." What im-
     presses in Auden's work is what is "individual" and most
     remote from any "comradeship." Auden's development in
     Marxist social criticism "looks unpleasantly like the end
     of Auden's talent."

14   TROY, WILLIAM. "Revolution by Poetic Justice." Nation, 144
     (27 March), 354-56.
          Auden along with Day Lewis, Michael Roberts, and Spender
     have embarrassed orthodox Marxists almost as much as they
     have the "bourgeois enemy against whom they wage guerilla
     warfare in their verse." Auden makes clearer what he
     opposes than what he supports, and critics have responded
     negatively either to his "shock tactics" or his "retreat
     into the private vision which amounts to something like
     religious backsliding." Auden and the others "are indulg-
     ing in the emotional satisfaction" without accepting "the
     moral and intellectual responsibilities involved" in com-
     munism as a dogma.

15   WALL, BERNARD. "W.H. Auden and Spanish Civilization." Colos-
     seum, 3 (September), 142-49.
          Three parts concern communism and Spain; a fourth and
     last part treats of Auden's poem Spain, in which the
     Marxist ideal and the middle-class ideal seem to become one.
     The point of view is that of the "foreign intellectual" pro-
     tested against by the Spanish revolutionaries. And these
     are far from middle-class since "they believe in systematic
     killing and say so." Revolutionary Spain is for Auden "a
     world in which he could not express himself."

16   WEYGANDT, CORNELIUS. "Of Poetry and Propaganda," in The Time
     of Yeats. New York: Appleton, pp. 429-33.
          Considers Auden the least of the trio that includes
     Spender and Day Lewis. Auden is principally a satirist and
     propagandist and has no poem that is worthy of being set

among "the best poems of our language." Weygandt lists a
good many of what he calls faults in Auden's verse, viz.:
"The schoolmaster in Auden breaks out now and then in little
pedantries and in passages of sesquipedalian words."

1938 A BOOKS - NONE

1938 B SHORTER WRITINGS

1   ANON. "W.H. Auden." Wilson Bulletin, 12 (January), 362.
        Biographical commentary on Auden's career. On Auden's
     receiving the King's Gold Medal in 1937, the writer says,
     "This award, by a conservative government, to a 'red' poet
     is perhaps the greatest of all indications that poetry in
     England is now standing on its own feet, and no longer
     needs the props of conventionality to win praise where
     praise is due."

2   BARNES, T.R. "Auden and Isherwood." Scrutiny, 7 (December),
     361-63.
        Negative review of On the Frontier as a tract with a
     clear but dull message. It lacks a plot, although things
     happen; the characters are mostly "from the stock wardrobe";
     and the dialogue is difficult and unbelievable.

3   DRUMMOND, JOHN. "The Mind of Mr. W.H. Auden." Townsman, 1
     (July), 23-26.
        Auden has no mind, only complexes. He is a guilt-ridden,
     semi-intellectual barbarian, who sometimes shows signs of
     an idea but overloads the signs with emotion so as to re-
     veal the idea as only pretense. Moreover, he is a coward
     with a death-wish, falsely romantic, and possessed of a
     false idealism that "leads him to believe that there is
     something morally wrong about personal forcefulness."

*4   DUDMAN, GEORGE, AND PATRICK TERRY. Challenge to Tom Harrison.
     Oxford, passim.
        Not seen. Cited in 1972.A2. Apparently has biographical
     information.

5   ENGLE, PAUL. "New English Poets." English Journal, college
     edition, 27 (February), 89-101.
        Auden is among the young poets who "restored to English
     poetry...hope without false cheerfulness and subject matter
     beyond the personal." On This Island "proves that writing
     can be intelligently didactic."

1938

6   FLINT, F. CUDWORTH. "New Leaders in English Poetry." Virginia
     Quarterly Review, 14 (Autumn), 502-18.
         Auden is one of the leaders of the young poets with "the
     new enthusiasm for psychoanalytic therapeutics and Marxian
     revolutionary economics." Criticism of Auden as one who
     never grew up may "be turned into a compliment...a way of
     saying that he has never finished growing." Describes
     Auden's style, subjects, and concerns; and concludes that
     his "distinctive importance" to modern poetry is in his use
     of materials deriving from Freud.

7   GLICKSBERG, C.I. "Poetry and Social Revolution." Dalhousie
     Review, 17 (January), 493-503.
         Replies to the Marxists' arguments that Auden, Spender,
     and Day Lewis have not been writing for the proletariat but
     for the intellectuals. Marxist criticism is absurd because
     it evaluates poets on the measure of their radicalism.
     Section 3 (498-500) treats Auden particularly and the set-
     ting forth of his diagnosis of society's ills. Only after
     the freedom of the individual is accomplished is it "possi-
     ble to set about rebuilding the broken foundations of our
     world." The modern poet, according to Glicksberg, faces
     the problem of what to believe in. Today his faith turns
     either to Catholicism or Communism.

*8   HEWETT, PETER. "W.H. Auden." University Forward, 4 (5 Feb-
     ruary), 5.
         Not seen. Cited in Bloomfield, 1972.A2.

9   IYENGAR, K.R. SRINIVASA. "Mr. W.H. Auden (The King's Poetry
     Medalist)." Journal of the University of Bombay, 6 (May),
     1-11.
         A summary of Auden's life, career, and praise for his
     poetry. Touches the influences on his technique and ideas,
     particularly Owen and Hopkins, with a long section on the
     special influence of Eliot. With Look, Stranger! and Spain
     Auden has left the tutelage of Eliot and has found his own
     voice. "He has now learned to achieve...the dual harmonies
     of the idea with the words, of the mind with the world."

10   MacNEICE, LOUIS. Modern Poetry. New York: Oxford Press,
     passim.
         The subtitle of the book A Personal Essay gives a clue
     to its contents. The first ninety pages or so are general
     about poetry and personal about MacNeice's responses to
     poetry and poets. From Chapter 6 MacNeice comments on
     Auden along with other poets under the headings "Imagery,"
     "Rhythm and Rhyme," "Diction," "Obscurity," and "Lighter
     Poetry and Drama." He believes that Auden has adopted

beliefs which he has "not yet quite grown into," but has not
stated his "beliefs more explicitly than is warranted by...
natural emotional reaction to them." Reprinted: 1969.B9.

11   SITWELL, EDITH. "Three Eras of Modern Poetry II," in Trio.
      London: Macmillan, pp. 177-85.
          Devotes a few paragraphs to Auden in this second lecture
      delivered in 1937 at the University of London. Directs her
      comments primarily at Day Lewis' claim of "a boom in
      poetry." Points out Auden's use of cliches in "Lay Your
      Sleeping Head, My Love"; labels him a "minor poet" though
      an "exquisite" one. Reprinted by Freeport Books for
      Libraries Press, 1970.

12   SOUTHWORTH, JAMES G. "Wystan Hugh Auden." Sewanee Review, 46
      (April-June), 189-205.
          Part I analyzes the "political theme" in Auden's poetry,
      Part II the personal theme, Part III the subjects, and
      Part IV the techniques. Auden's political problem "results
      from a sensitive person's impact with a reality which, be-
      cause of a defective social and educational system, he never
      dreamed existed." The personal and political attitudes are
      thus inseparable. Early in his work Auden sought "to cover
      beneath a cloak of studied smartness and sheer bravado a
      sense of guilt," which "pertness" he avoids in later lyrics
      in Look, Stranger! By his subjects, he "makes us see" the
      "conditions that cry aloud the necessity for change." He
      can communicate "all aspects of different emotional experi-
      ences by the perfect suitability of his prosodic form."
      Reprinted: 1940.B7.

13   SPENDER, STEPHEN. "The Poetic Dramas of W.H. Auden and
      Christopher Isherwood." New Writing, n.s. 1 (Autumn), 102-
      108.
          Auden and Isherwood proved they could write verse plays
      that attracted an audience large enough to warrant their
      staging but sacrificed their skill as poets; for their col-
      laboration produced works inferior to their individual ef-
      forts. The plays lose their effect by treating as absurd
      matters that really are absurd, "copying...directly from
      life." Lunatics listening approvingly to what Nazi leaders
      say, for example, produces complacency. Much is good in
      the plays, however; and Auden and Isherwood have begun to
      "solve the problems of creating a contemporary poetic
      drama."

1939

1939 A BOOKS - NONE

1939 B SHORTER WRITINGS

   1   ALLOTT, KENNETH. "A Tract." <u>New Verse</u>, n.s. 1 (January),
        24-25.
            Review of <u>On The Frontier</u>. Believes it oversimplified
        and trite and that Auden and Isherwood "have not exploited
        a tenth of their ability."

   2   BAILEY, RUTH. <u>A Dialogue on Modern Poetry</u>. London: Humphrey
        Milford, Oxford University Press, passim.
            Chooses two of Auden's poems to illustrate the controver-
        sy over whether modern poetry is sick or healthy. The dis-
        cussion is cast in the form of an overheard argument with
        an attacker, a defender, a plain reader, a moderator, etc.
        They discuss "Sir, no man's enemy, forgiving all" and "Song
        for the New Year."

   3   BROOKS, CLEANTH. <u>Modern Poetry and the Tradition</u>. Chapel Hill:
        University of North Carolina Press, pp. 125-35.
            "Auden represents...sensibility fortified with princi-
        ples...." He recovers "the archaic imagery...in the service
        of a fine irony." Discusses Auden's methods of contrast,
        assimilation and synthesis and his avoidance of didacticism,
        sentimentality, or oversimplification.

   4   DAICHES, DAVID. "W.H. Auden: The Search for a Public."
        <u>Poetry</u>, 54: 148-56.
            "To whom could a poet like Auden appeal?" The problem
        facing Auden (and all the younger poets of the post-war
        period) had two related parts: "what attitude?" and "which
        audience?" The early poems are confused on both these; with
        <u>The Orators</u> comes obscurity, followed by resolution in <u>On
        This Island</u>. He is addressing, says Daiches, "the ideal
        schoolboy." That is the person anxious about what he ob-
        serves in the present and is concerned about what to do for
        the future.

   5   EBERHART, RICHARD. "W.H. Auden." <u>We Moderns</u>: <u>Gotham Book
        Mart 1920-1940</u>. Catalogue 42, p. 12.
            Frances Steloff of the Gotham Book Mart requested from
        numerous writers a brief critical statement about other
        writers for her catalogue. Eberhart was assigned Auden.
        Auden's tragic flaw is Comedy; but "he has bottled up the
        atmosphere of a decade, presented us with an arch-especial
        drink." Lists Auden's works available at the Book Mart.

6   GRIGSON, GEOFFREY. "Remarks on Painting and Mr. Auden." New
    Verse, n.s. 1 (January), 17-19.
        Uses some remarks of Auden about art and Auden's praise
    of William Coldstream to begin an attack on Coldstream's
    paintings. Attacks Auden as well and anyone else who likes
    Coldstream.

7   _____. "Twenty-seven Sonnets." New Verse, n.s. 2 (May),
    47-49.
        Reviews "In Time of War" ("Sonnets from China"). Thinks
    this sonnet sequence the best poems in the last forty
    years. Auden "is something good and creative in European
    life in a time of the very greatest evil."

8   HAUSERMANN, H.W. "Left-wing Poetry: A Note." English
    Studies, 21 (October), 203-13 (esp. pp. 206-208).
        Discusses various poets as examples of the relationship
    of political creeds to aesthetic principles; describes the
    chief characteristics of the left-wing movement and its
    "historical relations to literary currents of the previous
    epoch." Auden protests "against tradition and the belief
    in tradition" in his early volumes where he had "advocated
    a change of heart, a renewal of the will." Communist ideas
    when they appear in his poetry particularize the enemy--
    "capitalism, high finance, militarism"--and make Auden's
    "poetical language" clearer.

9   HENDERSON, PHILIP. "The Auden Age," in The Poet and Society.
    London: Secker & Warburg, pp. 202-15.
        Finds Auden's poetry and plays trivial, fuzzy, and writ-
    ten "mainly for himself and his immediate friends." Com-
    ments on "The Orators," Poems, 1930, Paid on Both Sides,
    The Dance of Death, The Dog Beneath the Skin, and Look,
    Stranger! Generally a negative view of Auden's work as a
    kind of falling off from Eliot and Lawrence.

10 LEHMANN, JOHN. New Writing in England. New York: Critics
    Group Press, passim.
        Auden is only one of many examples of young writers
    after 1935 who became increasingly concerned with world
    politics. Only Auden's poems that related to Spain are
    treated, particularly, of course, Spain, which Lehmann con-
    siders "his richest and most concentrated single work up to
    date." A few scattered comments appear on other poems and
    a long paragraph on On the Frontier, pp. 35-36.

1939

11   SCHILLER, SISTER MARY B., O.S.F.   "Trends in Modern Poetic
        Drama in English, 1900-1938."   Ph.D. dissertation, Univer-
        sity of Illinois.
            Summarizes the plots of Auden's and Isherwood's plays
        and describes their salient features.   Praises their
        "originality, versatility, seriousness, humor, great power
        of satire and irony"; but finds the poets unable to pre-
        scribe a cure for the sick society they present and con-
        siders their philosophy "obscure, floundering, and inade-
        quate."   See pp. 230-42.

12   SCHWARTZ, DELMORE.   "The Two Audens."   Kenyon Review, 1 (Win-
        ter), 34-45.
            Studies the "conjunction of Freud and Marx" in Auden.
        One Auden is "the clever guy..., the popular entertainer,
        propagandist, and satirist...."   Schwartz calls the voice of
        this Auden, "the Ego," and "then the other voice will have
        to be called the Id."   He treats these terms as relevant
        critical terms and not clinical, Freudian terms by applying
        them briefly to a few selections from Auden's books into
        1938.   Reprinted: 1970.B19.

13   SPENDER, STEPHEN.   "The Importance of W.H. Auden."   London
        Mercury, 39 (April), 613-18.
            Auden's importance is that "he is one of the poets who
        is interpreting the events of our immediate life to us"
        and not that he is important to the tradition of English
        poetry.   Spender lists and describes Auden's qualities as a
        writer and as a person as well as his contributions to the
        technique of modern poetry.

14   SYMONS, JULIAN.   "Auden and Poetic Drama 1938."   Life and
        Letters Today, 20 (February), 70-79.
            Sees Auden's plays as an unsuccessful attempt "to recon-
        cile Eliot's ideas with his own."   Thinks On the Frontier
        of most merit.   Symons judges the "poetic playwright" from
        the standpoint of competition "on one level with Mr. Noel
        Coward and Mr. Robert E. Sherwood and on another with
        Sophocles and Shakespeare."

1940 A BOOKS - NONE

1940 B SHORTER WRITINGS

1   APPEL, BENJAMIN.   "The Exiled Writers."   Saturday Review of
        Literature, 22 (19 October), 3-5, 14 (esp. p. 5).
            Question and answer interview with Auden about his atti-
        tudes toward America, his plans, and his work on Paul Bunyan.

2   DAICHES, DAVID. "Into the World." Poetry, 56 (April), 40-43.
        A review of Another Time. Compares Another Time with
    Auden's Poems and sees a trailing off from the previous
    volume. At the same time "it has more promise." Attri-
    butes some of the falling off to Auden's relocation in
    America; he is no longer looking at England, but at the
    world, "a larger and a more horrible domain."

3   _____. "Poetry in the 1930's: II. W.H. Auden and
    Stephen Spender," in Poetry and the Modern World.
    Chicago: University of Chicago Press, pp. 214-39.
        Describes and judges in a general way Auden's poetry
    from 1930 to 1939, the technique, influences, points of
    view, and themes. The Orators is the most difficult book
    for ordinary readers because it is obscure. Early con-
    flicts seem resolved in Look, Stranger! "at least tem-
    porarily," and Auden has not made "poetic progress" since
    then.

4   LEHMANN, JOHN. New Writing in Europe. Harmondsworth:
    Penguin, passim.
        Discusses the development of Auden's work along with
    the works of other writers in the thirties who Lehmann
    feels were more socially, politically, and morally con-
    scious than most. Their role they themselves saw as
    interpreting "the social, political, and moral changes"
    of the thirties "to the widest possible circles of or-
    dinary people...." See especially chapters 2, 4, and the
    beginning of 7.

5   MUIR, EDWIN. "Recent Poetry." Purpose, 12 (July-December),
    149-52 (especially pp. 150-51).
        A brief review of Another Time, commenting especially
    on Auden's use of epithets. These imply intellectual
    comment that interferes with the "profound and beautiful"
    feeling in his poems.

6   ORWELL, GEORGE. Inside the Whale. London: Gollancz, pp.
    169-70.
        Says "Spain 1937" is "one of the few decent things that
    have been written about the Spanish War." Orwell criti-
    cizes the phrase "necessary murder" (as does Auden later)
    as "written by a person to whom murder is at most a word."
    Reprinted: 1968.B10.

7   SOUTHWORTH, JAMES G. "Wystan Hugh Auden," in Sowing the
    Spring. Oxford: Blackwell, pp. 128-48.
        Reprint of 1938.B11.

W. H. AUDEN: A REFERENCE GUIDE

1940

8   WELLS, HENRY W. New Poets from Old. New York: Columbia
    University Press, pp. 46-49, 63-70, passim.
        Examines influence of medieval literature on Auden and
    his changes in style and political philosophy. Auden
    shows little indebtedness to Beowulf but familiarity with
    Langland and Chaucer; he turns from the romantic tradition
    towards the late Middle Ages in style and themes. Com-
    pares the colloquial style of a passage from The Reeve's
    Tale with a passage from The Dog Beneath the Skin. This
    change in style accompanies change in political philosophy
    from "philandering with autocratic and aristocratic the-
    ories of government" to "a radical view of society."

1941 A   BOOKS - NONE

1941 B   SHORTER WRITINGS

1   BRENNER, RICA. "Wystan Hugh Auden," in Poets of Our Time.
    New York: Harcourt, Brace, pp. 245-77.
        General introduction to Auden for young readers, with a
    brief biography of his early years and a biographical,
    critical account of his verse. Asserts that "in Auden's
    philosophic belief, is a key to that quality that has been
    noted in his poetry--the close coupling of the private and
    public, the personal and the impersonal."

2   BULLOUGH, GEOFFREY. "Metaphysicals and Left-Wingers," in
    The Trend of Modern Poetry. Edinburgh: Oliver & Boyd,
    pp. 165-69.
        Reprint of 1934.B1.

3   COWLEY, MALCOM. "Auden in America." New Republic, 104 (7
    April), 473-74.
        A review of The Double Man, touching on Auden's philo-
    sophical background. Calls The Double Man "an unfamiliar
    and uncomfortable but stimulating world of ideas," a moral
    poem, rather than a political one. Cowley thinks Auden's
    brand of morality which fails to recognize degrees of guilt
    (on the principle that all men are sinners) may lead
    "into an attitude of pure passivity."

4   DEUTSCH, BABETTE. "Sirs, What Must I Do To Be Saved?"
    Poetry, 58: 148-52.
        A review of The Double Man. Auden seems to have given
    up his hope expressed in an earlier poem "for a change of
    heart" and has settled instead for "new styles of archi-
    tecture." Auden is "sharply aware of human ambivalence...,
    and it is with painful cognizance of the difficulties

18

involved that he demands that we set our house in order...."
Deutsch likes the poem better "as ethics than as verse."

5   JARRELL, RANDALL. "Changes of Attitude and Rhetoric in
     Auden's Poetry." The Southern Review, 7: 326-49.
         Part 1 analyzes "the general position Auden makes for
     himself in his early poems" (apparently a position com-
     piled of Marx, Freud and Groddeck, the folk, sciences,
     boyhood, and homosexuality), and shows how the different
     position of the later poems grew from it. Part 2 describes
     Auden's language and rhetoric. The judgments are mostly
     unkind, and Jarrell concludes, "But analyses, even unkind
     analyses of faults, are one way of showing apprecia-
     tion...." Reprinted: 1969.B6.

6   ____. "The Double Man." Nation, 152 (12 April), 440-
     41.
         A favorable review of The Double Man and "New Year
     Letter." Auden "has accomplished the entirely unexpected
     feat of making a successful long poem out of a reasonable,
     objective, and comprehensive discussion."

7   TATE, ALLEN. "Understanding Modern Poetry," in Reason in
     Madness. New York: Putnam, pp. 97-98.
         Tate concludes this chapter with a brief comment on
     "Our Hunting Fathers" that the complications of metaphor
     "can be returned without confusion or contradiction to a
     definite, literal, and coherent field of imagery"; that
     Auden extends meaning by this field. All the implications
     refer to the hunting squire who "becomes predatory man."

8   WINKLER, R.O.C. "Mr. Auden's Weltanschauung." Scrutiny, 10
     (2 October), 206-11.
         A generally negative review of New Year Letter. Winkler
     finds it simple-minded and written so as to "hang a cur-
     tain between author and reader." Praises the Prologue as
     closer to Auden's earlier work and recommends that later
     editions should omit the Letter and the notes.

1942 A BOOKS - NONE

1942 B SHORTER WRITINGS

1   SCARFE, FRANCIS. Auden and After: The Liberation of Poetry,
     1930-1941. London: Routledge, passim (especially pp.
     10-34).

1942

       Assessment of Auden as an "important poet" but not a "great" one. Contains a section of comparison with other poets of the time, one on Auden's psychology, on politics, and one on style. Sees Auden as still a developing poet.

1944 A   BOOKS - NONE

1944 B   SHORTER WRITINGS

1   DUPEE, F.W. "W.H. Auden." The Nation, 159 (28 October), 537-38.
       A review of For the Time Being. It "is the work of a great and serious poet." Within "conventional adaptation of the philosophical poem...Auden has given amazing life to the old business of choruses and semi-choruses and talking abstractions."

2   FREMANTLE, ANNE. "Wise Man's Sons." Commonweal, 41 (8 December), 194-98.
       A review of For the Time Being. Finds that Auden's verse uses a current idiom "as did Chaucer and Shakespeare" compared to Milton, Joyce, and Eliot, whose language is "remote from current usage." The verse has an "undercurrent of gaiety" though "there is nothing local or insular." Both poems "are scholarly and thoughtful" and "intuitively profound" about how we lie to ourselves and how stupid we are. Auden's superiority "probably owes a good deal to his capacity for accepting."

3   GREGORY, HORACE. "Of Vitality, Regionalism, and Satire in Recent American Poetry." Sewanee Review, 52 (Fall), 579-83.
       In spite of the presence of the ephemeral slang, colloquialisms, and private jokes, Auden's poetry will endure because it "exists--and with appropriate freedom and wit-- within the tradition of English lyric verse." Gregory considers Richard Lovelace to be Auden's literary ancestor.

4   LEVIN, HARRY. "Through the Looking Glass." The New Republic, 111 (18 September, 347-48.
       A review of For the Time Being. Observes that in both "The Sea and the Mirror" and "For the Time Being" there is "a narcissistic tendency to escape through the looking glass into an island kingdom or desert exile." They present "a sentimental notion of culture and a naive prejudice against science...."

5 SAVAGE, D.S. "The Strange Case of W.H. Auden," in <u>The Per-</u>
     <u>sonal Principle</u>. London: Routledge, pp. 155-82.
        Auden's work attempts "escape from personality into a
     real, objective social world, which in truth has no exist-
     ence." Consequently, it "shows increasing tenuousness and
     fantasy: instead of a realization of experience it reveals
     a dissipation through poetic disintegration." Savage
     believes a "literal disintegration" occurred in Auden's
     work and marks the "first sign" as a "fissure between the
     solemn and the farcical elements in his work," to wit, in
     <u>Look, Stranger!</u>; "<u>New Year Letter</u> shows Auden's final ab-
     dication as a poet." Repeats most of Savage's opinions ex-
     pressed in 1944.B6. Reprinted: 1969.B12.

6 _____. "The Poet's Perspectives." <u>Poetry</u>, 64 (June),
     148-58.
        Thinks Auden is the least gifted, least interesting,
     and most deteriorated of the three poets, Auden, Spender,
     and MacNeice. "Auden reached the limit of his achievement
     in his first book" and indeed all three are failures,
     "equivalent to a failure of personality"; and although
     earnest and sincere, they are superficial and have sepa-
     rated themselves "from the depths of being."

1945 A   BOOKS - NONE

1945 B   SHORTER WRITINGS

1 COWLEY, MALCOLM. "Virtue and Virtuosity: Notes on W.H.
     Auden." <u>Poetry</u>, 65 (January), 202-209.
        A review of <u>For the Time Being</u>. Auden without equal in
     technical skill among contemporary English and American
     poets. Analyzes this skill, particularly the rhymes, "the
     greatest of technical difficulties" in English, and as-
     serts that Auden solves such problems with "easy grace."
     Offers clues to help explain allusions in these poems such
     as, "Original Sin is always equivalent to self-pride or
     narcissism...."

2 DUPEE, F.W. "Auden and Others." <u>Nation</u>, 160 (26 May), 605-
     606.
        A review of <u>The Collected Poetry</u>, which challenges
     Auden's own modest assessment of himself and praises the
     volume. "This collection certainly confirms Auden's great
     reputation." The "Others" in the essay are "young and
     unheard-of poets" who are remotely connected in Dupee's
     mind with the Auden-Spender group.

1945

3 FREMANTLE, ANNE. "Auden's Odyssey." Commonweal, 42 (25 May),
    141-43.
        A review of The Collected Poetry. Describes and as-
    sesses this book as a definite stage in Auden's reputation
    and career; thinks Auden has attempted to forestall any-
    one's tracing a development by arranging the poems alpha-
    betically by first lines; makes admiring comments on
    Auden's skill at separating the lyric and the satire, on
    his keeping his verse and prose separate (as in "The Sea
    and the Mirror"), on the literary criticism in his poems
    on poets" and the "advance" over "the doggerel of...'Jour-
    ney to a War,' and even some of 'The Orators' and the
    'New Year Letter'...."

4 HAMM, VICTOR M. "W.H. Auden: Pilgrim's Regress?" America,
    73 (26 May), 156-57.
        Summarizes Auden's poetic works with a brief descriptive
    commentary on each; labels For the Time Being "the first
    explicitly and authentically Christian poem Auden has
    written"; and concludes that it "demonstrates...that the
    poet has definitely got clear of the Waste Land of agnos-
    ticism."

5 JARRELL, RANDALL. "From Freud to Paul: The Stages of Auden's
    Ideology." Partisan Review, 12 (Fall), 437-57.
        Part I divides Auden's work into three entirely dis-
    tinct stages. Stage I "is the world of the unconscious,
    the primitive, the childish, the animal, the natural: it
    is Genesis." In Stage II, "Existence has become a problem
    that Auden reasons about...." To Stage III Jarrell gives
    the name "Paul," wherein Auden tells us that "no works can
    either save us or make us worth saving." Part II of the
    essay reintegrates Auden's work of the three stages as
    products of his feelings of guilt and anxiety. Part III
    concludes that Auden has projected a paradigm of his "self"
    upon the universe. Reprinted: 1969.B5.

6 LECHLITNER, RUTH. "The Odyssey of Auden." Poetry, 66 (July),
    204-15.
        A review of The Collected Poetry. Auden is more inter-
    ested in "the human thing" than in nature: "From the
    human scene in wartime come his most vivid images." Col-
    lected Poetry reveals more about Auden's craftsmanship
    than about the development of his ideas, though the omis-
    sions "may be as important to an understanding of his de-
    velopment as what he includes." Compares the present work
    with the earlier work and sees his individual works as
    signposts of his "odyssey."

7   NORTON, DAN S. "Auden's Poetry." <u>Virginia Quarterly Review</u>,
    21 (Summer), 434-41.
        A review of <u>The Collected Poetry</u>. Auden's achievement
    of the forties compares with Eliot's of the twenties.
    Norton contrasts what he calls Auden's positive affirmation
    with Eliot's negative affirmation. They "both plot the
    contours of the ruined city" but Eliot "speaks as an anti-
    quarian," Auden as one "who wants a house to live in...."
    Auden employs one kind of image "that gives form to con-
    cepts" and another that synthesizes "the shapes of dark-
    ness" and "gives form...to man's unconscious drives."

8   SHAPIRO, KARL. <u>Essay on Rime</u>. New York: Reynall & Hitch-
    cock, pp. 18-19, 41-44.
        Claims Auden has dominated English and American verse
    since 1935 and examines his vocabulary as a good influence
    and his practice of abstraction as "one pernicious influ-
    ence of his style."

<u>1946 A   BOOKS - NONE</u>

<u>1946 B   SHORTER WRITINGS</u>

1   GREGORY, HORACE, AND MARYA ZATURENSKA. "Epilogue: Recent
    American Poetry," in <u>A History of American Poetry, 1900-
    1940</u>. New York: Harcourt, Brace, pp. 483-96 (especially
    487-90).
        Tries to answer the question of the endurance of Auden's
    verse by listing its strengths and comparing Auden to
    D.H. Lawrence (in the creation of a literary personality)
    and to Richard Lovelace (as Auden's literary ancestor).

2   MILES, JOSEPHINE. "Major Adjectives in Poetry: from Wyatt
    to Auden." <u>University of California Publications in
    English</u>, 12, 3 (February), 305-426 (especially 398-99).
        Auden receives only two pages in this long essay, al-
    though a few other brief mentionings occur. Auden's use
    of adjectives is compared with that of Eliot and Yeats,
    placing him firmly in the "modern" since he uses fewer
    epithets than Hopkins or Whitman.

3   MIZNER, ARTHUR. "Ideas in Auden," in <u>Accent Anthology</u>. New
    York: Harcourt, Brace, pp. 630-35.
        Auden deals in <u>For the Time Being</u> with two problems,
    first in "The Sea and the Mirror" with "the relation of
    the artist's imagination to reality" and then in "For the
    Time Being" with "reality's relation to actuality." Offers

1946

a brief commentary on the working out or presentation of
these ideas.

4 [MORRISON, CHARLES C.] "The Faith of W.H. Auden." The Christian Century, 63 (16 January), 71-73.
Sees Auden's coming to the United States as a turning
point. Auden "has deliberately turned his back on the
sharp social satire of his earlier verse...." Declares
that Auden's current work is an "index to the vigor and
power of Christian faith...."

5 SPENDER, STEPHEN. "W.H. Auden and the Poets of the Thirties."
in Poetry Since 1939. London: Longmans, Green, pp. 28-33.
Published for the British (Arts) Council primarily to
answer the question "What poems have been written between
1939 and 1945 in Britain?" Chapter 9 describes and judges
Auden's poems, particularly New Year Letter and The Sea and
the Mirror: "the didactic, highly intellectualised, technically dazzling, at times wise poetry of an aloof com-
mentator, endowed with great cleverness and a lucid gift."
Compares Auden to Kipling in power of improvisation, use
of many forms, mastery of idiom and modern techniques,
familiarity with technical jargon, and a quality Spender
calls "a certain elusiveness." We may know and mark "the
Audenesque mood and the Audenesque attitude...but not...
Auden." Reprinted: 1948.B12; 1949.B12; 1970.B22.

6 STAFFER, DONALD A. "Which Side Am I Supposed to Be On?"
Virginia Quarterly Review, 22 (Autumn), 570-80.
Subtitled "The Search for Beliefs in W.H. Auden's
Poetry." Partly biographical and partly literary analysis,
fits Auden into the world between wars and follows the influences on his changing beliefs as reflected in his
literary work. Auden believes "that all men are sinful,
and that all men are brothers." These two beliefs "explain
Auden's inevitable drift toward the Christian faith."

7 WASSON, S. CARSON. "A Descant on W.H. Auden's Christmas
Oratorio." Crozer Quarterly, 23 (October), 340-49.
Analysis of Auden's "last poem--and his greatest."
Describes briefly Auden's career and the tenor of his
"growth" towards affirming "the Christian faith." Sum-
marizes and comments on the action of "For the Time Being"
and concludes that Auden "has outgrown most of his
cynicism."

W. H. Auden: A Reference Guide

1947

1947 A BOOKS - NONE

1947 B SHORTER WRITINGS

1   BROOKS, BENJAMIN GILBERT. "The Poetry of W.H. Auden." Nine-
    teenth Century and After, 141 (January, 30-40).
        Auden has managed to transmute everyday language, the
    journalistic, the technical into poetry, into images having
    "a fresh, relatively simple, unexpected beauty...." Traces
    the development of Auden's attitudes (he "adopted no con-
    sistent attitude") from Poems (1930) to For the Time Being,
    marking changes on the way. All this prepares for analysis
    of "The Sea and the Mirror" and "For the Time Being."

2   ELTON, WILLIAM. "Metapoetry by a Thinking Type." Poetry, 71
    (November), 90-94.
        Negative review of The Age of Anxiety. "Mr. Auden's
    importance is less as an artist than as the supreme broken
    record of Zeitgeist." After listing Auden's faults and
    confessing surprise at Auden's significance, Elton con-
    cludes "conceptual brilliance and an occasional felicitous
    passage are bound up with a false poetic theory, accounting
    for the paradox of his position...."

3   GRIFFIN, HOWARD. "The Idiom of W.H. Auden." New Quarterly
    of Poetry, 2 (Fall), 6-10.
        Enumerates aspects of Auden's style, which make up his
    "idiom": detachment (at the center but apart), use of ex-
    ternal scenes as metaphors for moral systems, multiform
    attacks on problems, functional use of metaphor or simile,
    evocative vocal effects, Spenserian props, an "action-
    hero" theme, and in the English tradition "a sort of
    dazzling nonchalance."

4   ISHERWOOD, CHRISTOPHER. Lions and Shadows. Norfolk, Connec-
    ticut: New Directions, pp. 181-229, passim.
        Autobiography of Isherwood to age twenty-five, not en-
    tirely disguised as a novel; uses fictitious names for his
    acquaintances. Chapter 5 contains a "caricature" of Auden
    under the name of Hugh Weston, and the character continues
    as part of Isherwood's life and education to the end of the
    book.

5   JAMESON, STORM. "W.H. Auden, the Poet of Angst." Gate
    (Oxford), 1 (December), 2-9.
        Jameson explains Auden's migration to America when
    England is on the verge of war by seeing the move as "with-
    drawal," the creative artist preserving his future works.

25

1947

The Angst points towards Auden's concern with the nature
of man, and Jameson's discussion unfolds this theme from
the early poems to The Age of Anxiety, finds technical but
no spiritual development, and describes weaknesses in
Auden's craft and thoughts and some of his strengths.
Reprinted: 1948.B6; 1950.B5.

6   JARRELL, RANDALL. "Verse Chronicle." The Nation, 165 (18
     October), 424-25.
          Half of this review is on The Age of Anxiety (p. 424),
     which Jarrell believes "the worst thing Auden has written
     since 'The Dance of Death.'" He complains most about "the
     same old voice saying the same old thing.... You might as
     well give yourself room for completely free association."
     He nevertheless believes Auden "was, and is potentially,
     one of the best poets on earth...."

1948 A BOOKS - NONE

1948 B SHORTER WRITINGS

1   BLOOMFIELD, MORTON W. "'Doom is Dark and Deeper Than Any
     Sea-dingle': W.H. Auden and Sawle's Warde." Modern
     Language Notes, 63 (December), 548-52.
          Weighs the similarities and differences between Auden's
     poem and his source. The poem is "far from the spirit of
     Sawle's Warde," but retains the impress of Auden's earlier
     reading and studying. "...Remembering that Auden nosed
     'among Saxon skulls, roots of our genealogies' will aid us
     in the fuller comprehension of the body of his poetry and
     of his methods of composing...."

2   BRADBURY, JOHN M. "Auden and the Tradition." Western Review,
     12 (Summer), 223-29.
          Auden was a tentative poet until The Collected Poems
     (1945). He committed himself with that publication to "an
     aesthetic and intellectual position." It showed "a
     serious, ...consistent artist, dedicated to broadening and
     opening to a freer, more public air and poetic tradition
     which Yeats and Eliot had created." From this point and
     in this respect Bradbury compares Auden's work to that of
     Yeats and Eliot. Auden by striving to treat man's situa-
     tion in dramatic terms has demonstrated that "twentieth
     century poetry need not continue to develop in the di-
     rection of self-absorption and private cabbalism."

3   COGHILL, NEVILL. "Sweeney Agonistes," In <u>T.S. Eliot: A Symposium</u>. Edited by Richard March and Tambimuttu. London: Poetry London, p. 82.
      Brief anecdote on Auden's early response to Eliot. Auden tore up all his poems because they were based on Wordsworth and "wouldn't do nowadays." Reprinted: 1949.B5.

4   DUNCAN, CHESTER. "W.H. Auden." <u>Canadian Forum</u>, 28 (September), 131-32.
      Of the courses open to the modern poet, to treat what he knows or to explore "the whole amazing panorama," Auden has chosen "the dangerous second." Although he fails occasionally, he mostly succeeds; for "he is a stylist of range and delicacy." His interest in morality directs him, even in describing the panorama, in all his subjects "to make public meaning out of his private spirit." Predicts that Auden will do as much in the next twenty years as he has in the past twenty; "like Shakespeare's, his technique is always catching up to his thought...."

5   GREENBERG, SAMUEL. "W.H. Auden: Poet of Anxiety." <u>Masses and Mainstream</u>, 1 (June), 38-50.
      Tries to dispel the "Myth" that Auden "has grown as a poet and thinker," that "he was a Marxist and is now a liberal," that in his "class ambiguities" there is "artistic strength." A book by book account of failure to find any of these (to <u>The Age of Anxiety</u>).

6   JAMESON, STORM. "W.H. Auden, the Poet of <u>Angst</u>." <u>Gate</u> (Oxford), 2: 17-24.
      Reprint of 1947.B5.

7   KERMODE, FRANK. "The Theme of Auden's Poetry: I." <u>Revista di Letterature Moderne e Comparate</u>, 3 (March-June), 1-14.
      Auden's major theme concerns poetry, the poet, and the relation of both to society. Kermode discusses the verse up to <u>The Age of Anxiety</u>, including techniques and subjects. He gives special attention to the problem of obscurity, seeing in Auden's allusions a degree of snobbishness, and also attempts to clarify some of the obscure passages.

8   LEINHARDT, R.G. "Auden's Inverted Development," in <u>The Importance of Scrutiny</u>. Edited by Eric Bentley. New York: G.W. Stewart, pp. 249-54.
      A negative view of Auden. He started out with extraordinary talent, and occasionally that talent surfaces in places in <u>For the Time Being.</u> His greatest problem "lies

1948

in determining quite what he wishes to express and in
formulating an appropriate attitude towards it...."

9 MASON, H.A. "Mr. Auden's Quartet." Scrutiny, 15 (Spring),
155-60.
Auden's review of The Age of Anxiety. One may "admire
the breadth and range of reference...the discovery of a
form which makes a virtue out of the characteristic weaknesses.... Yet is is with disappointment...one reflects on
the absence of any spark of vitality...."

10 MASON, RONALD. "W.H. Auden," in Writers of Today, vol. 2.
Edited by Denys Val Baker. London: Sidgwick & Jackson,
pp. 105-16.
A general commentary on Auden and his work. Spain (1937)
marks a change in Auden's consciousness from "sardonic
detachment" to one producing a poetry that "was at last
inspired by the condition of men rather than by the condition of Auden." Mason traces some backsliding in New Year
Letter that may have been cathartic as he goes on to examine the new strain in The Sea and the Mirror and other
poems.

11 SPENDER, STEPHEN. "The Life of Literature." Partisan Review,
15: 1311-31.
The second part of an autobiography of Spender; mentions
Auden's influence or effect on him and his ideas about
"modern" poetry.

12 _____. "W.H. Auden and the Poets of the Thirties," in
Poetry Since 1939. London: Longmans, Green, pp. 28-33.
Reprint of 1946.B5.

1949 A BOOKS

1 SCARFE, FRANCIS. W.H. Auden. Contemporary British Poets
Series. Monaco: Lyrebird Press, 69 pp.
A biographical and critical account of Auden and his
work, describing what Scarfe thinks the best and worst
poems in a given collection and including some account of
the critical reception through The Age of Anxiety. Does
not contain a bibliography or index. The general theme
is "Auden the synthesizer." Reprinted: 1971.A3.

1949 B SHORTER WRITINGS

1 ANDERSON, D.M. "Aspects of Auden." Landfall, 3 (September),
270-79.
Auden's concern in New Year Letter is chiefly with the

problem of order and related to it, the nature of art. There
follows further observations on the manifestation of this
concern in The Sea and the Mirror and For the Time Being.
The "Christmas Oratorio" is seen as performing the same
function for Christ's incarnation as The Sea and the Mirror
for The Tempest.

2   BEACH, JOSEPH WARREN. "Poems of Auden and Prose Diathesis."
     Virginia Quarterly Review, 25 (July), 365-83.
        Auden's "poems illustrate the wide range from one end to
     the other of the prose-poetry spectrum." Beach raises the
     question of Auden's mixing the two so far as "to defeat his
     own artistic aims." As answer he tabulates the greater
     number of poems in The Collected Poetry (1945) as abstract
     and discursive dressed in verse forms. On this thesis rest
     descriptions of Auden's poems through The Age of Anxiety
     and New Year Letter and Beach's judgment of their success:
     "...for undertakings so delicate and complicated, he has
     not demonstrated the possession of an infallible touchstone
     of taste."

3   BULLOUGH, GEOFFREY. "Metaphysicals and Left-Wingers," in The
     Trend of Modern Poetry. Edinburgh: Oliver & Boyd, pp.
     188-96.
        Commentary up to For the Time Being and to what he calls
     Auden's "semi-religious position." Revised edition of
     1941.B2.

4   CHASE, RICHARD VOLNEY. Quest for Myth. Baton Rouge: Louisi-
     ana State University Press, pp. 127-31.
        Considers poets mythmakers and uses Auden's poem "In
     Sickness and in Health" to demonstrate that poetry strug-
     gles "against human bias and exclusiveness to transfigure
     itself into myth." Offers a close reading with this
     thesis in mind.

5   COGHILL, NEVILL. "Sweeney Agonistes," in T.S. Eliot: A
     Symposium. Edited by Richard March and Tambimuttu.
     Chicago: Henry Regnery and Co., p. 82.
        Reprint of 1948.B3.

6   FRANKENBERG, LLOYD. "W.H. Auden," in Pleasure Dome. Boston:
     Houghton Mifflin, pp. 301-15.
        A running commentary on most of Auden's more frequently
     anthologized pieces and two longer poems, "New Year Letter"
     and "For the Time Being": "Law Like Love" crosses Kafka
     with A.A. Milne, "New Year Letter" is "probably the finest
     long purely didactic poem of our time," and "For the Time
     Being" could have been "a commentary on Eliot's plays and

Four Quartets." All of Auden's poetry is "a symbol...of
the disharmonies of our age, and a search for their reso-
lution."

7   GRIFFIN, HOWARD. "Conversation on Cornelia St.: A Dialogue
     with W.H. Auden." Accent, 10 (Autumn), 51-58.
          Conversation about morality, the role and function of
     the artist, and the nature of mankind. "The Garden of
     Eden idea serves to remind human beings that they are
     fallible and have to be redeemed."

8   HAMILTON, G. ROSTREVOR. The Tell-tale Article. London:
     Heinemann, pp. 40-50, passim.
          Auden shares with Eliot the distinction among modern
     poets of using the definite article most frequently (about
     ten percent of the total words). Such usage for Hamilton
     means "a weakness in structure, a degeneration of syntax."
     While Eliot departs "from normal usage," he does less
     violence to syntax than does Auden, who is "not only ob-
     scure, but wantonly obscure." In "Spain" Hamilton finds
     that the definite article equals twenty percent (151 times
     in 744 words)--"the degeneration of syntax could hardly
     go further." This overuse, symptomatic of modern verse,
     represents a lack "of the sense of man's greatness," in
     contrast to former times.

9   McCOARD, WILLIAM B. "An Interpretation of the Times: A
     Report on the Oral Interpretation of W.H. Auden's 'Age of
     Anxiety.'" Quarterly Journal of Speech, 35 (December),
     489-95.
          Argues for oral interpretation as a way for poetry to
     "reach highest communicative, artistic power..." and
     describes the preparations for presentation of The Age of
     Anxiety. "The oral interpreter...has the responsibility
     of selecting that which is essential" (to be delivered in
     one hour). Instructs readers in techniques of making ideas
     dramatic. Includes the program notes that accompanied
     actual performances, notes on the plot and style of the
     poem, on Auden, and on the nature of poetic facts. Con-
     cludes with the introduction given orally at the perform-
     ances and a comment on the audience reaction.

10   REXROTH, KENNETH. "Introduction," in New British Poets. New
     York: New Directions, passim.
          A general essay on modern poetry beginning with Auden
     and his "circle." Discusses Auden's influence on his
     contemporaries and its gradual fading away and giving place
     to Dylan Thomas.

W. H. Auden: A Reference Guide

11   SPENDER, STEPHEN. "The Life of Literature." <u>Partisan Review</u>,
      16: 56-66.
         The third part of Spender's autobiographical work in
      progress. Mentions Auden but describes Spender's experi-
      ences with other writers of the time more than his ac-
      quaintance with Auden.

12   _____. "W.H. Auden and the Poets of the Thirties," in
      <u>Poetry Since 1939</u>. London: Longmans, Green, pp. 28-33.
         Reprint of 1948.B12.

13   _____. "W.H. Auden at Oxford." <u>World Review</u>, n.s. 6
      (August), 45-49.
         Auden's supreme confidence demonstrates itself in his
      ability to fit himself as well as everyone else into a
      pattern that represents the whole of life. This talent is
      anti-romantic, rather than romantic, and Auden possesses
      it to an extraordinary degree. Imparts numerous details
      and anecdotes of Spender's acquaintance with Auden at
      Oxford, where Auden had already made himself a legend be-
      fore Spender's arrival. Some of the anecdotes make Auden
      seem rude as well as eccentric.

14   WHITE, ERIC WALTER. "Collaboration with W.H. Auden," in
      <u>Benjamin Britten</u>. London: Boosey & Hawkes, pp. 8-12.
         Hints at some effects on Auden of his friendship with
      Britten, but the book is about Britten and therefore the
      effects of this friendship on him. Some biographical com-
      ments on Auden and some on his intentions in his works
      written for and with Britten. Reprinted: 1970.B26.

1950 A   BOOKS - NONE

1950 B   SHORTER WRITINGS

1   BARKER, GEORGE. "Reviews of Books: Collected Shorter Poems,
     W.H. Auden." <u>Life and Letters</u>, 65 (April-June), 68-70.
        The subject of the poet is "the business of being alive,"
     and Auden has illustrated in <u>Collected Shorter Poems</u> that
     writing poetry is his natural function. Barker discusses
     also the nature of poetic knowledge as implied by Auden's
     contention that "all knowledge that conflicts with itself
     is Poetic Fiction."

2   BARZUN, JACQUES. "Auden on Romanticism." <u>Yale Review</u>, 39
     (June), 730-33.

31

1950

A review of The Enchafèd Flood. Auden sees in the Romantic longing for the sea "a rejection, or at least a condemnation, of the city, that is, of society." Man's task now is to build a new city, not "to explore unknown wastes." Auden omits the Romantics from 1820 to 1850 and several apparent favorites of Barzun. Since Auden did not pretend to be exhaustive in three essays, says Barzun, "may he...give us the complete symphony in four movements."

3 FRASER, G.S. "Notes on the Achievement of Auden," in his Post-War Trends in English Literature. Tokyo: Hokuseido, pp. 51-63.
   Summary of Auden's thought from his early belief that history itself is redemptive to his assertion that "we must love one another or die" and of his style from the "curt and elliptical and therefore often rather obscure" to a "loose and free technique...of the urgent but spontaneous tone of excited speech." Fraser thinks Auden, in spite of the Christian point of view, indifferent to rather than detached from "human feelings"; that he has developed a tone of "facetiousness" as a defense against an accusation of having a conventional attitude. Auden is therefore more interested in general cases than in persons.

4 GREENBERG, MARTIN. "Auden as Critic." Nation, 170 (29 April), 407-408.
   Auden writes about romanticism rather conventionally, offering neither the new nor the unexpected. Discusses Auden's method in The Enchafèd Flood, which Auden subtitled "An Iconography."

5 JAMESON, STORM. "W.H. Auden, the Poet of Angst," in his The Writer's Situation. London: MacMillan, pp. 83-101.
   Reprint of 1948.B6.

1951 A BOOKS

1 HOGGART, RICHARD. Auden: An Introductory Essay. New Haven: Yale University Press, 256 pp.
   Hoggart's intention is to address the literary layman who is interested "in the quality of our lives today, and a readiness to examine whether the reading of poetry has an important relation to that interest." The discussion is arranged generally from Auden's early work to the later (1950). Hoggart thinks of this book as an introduction, "a running of the finger down certain aspects of Auden's verse." Most critics think of this work as the first of the best criticisms of Auden.

W. H. Auden: A Reference Guide

1951 B SHORTER WRITINGS

1   CARRUTH, HAYDEN. "Public Poems." Nation, 172 (2 June), 524-25.
    In contrast to the personal voice, Nones offers the point of view "We," meaning that part of the public that "notices and deplores...our destructive society." Auden is a satirist who exercises the same kind of control as Swift, who like Byron turns anxiety and guilt "to the satirist's account." All the poems display "genuine feeling and craftsmanship."

2   _____. "Understanding Auden." Nation, 173 (22 December), 550-51.
    Review of Hoggart's Auden: An Introductory Essay (1951.A1). In preparation for his review Carruth read most of Auden's writings "at one stretch," partly to see what the critical problems are. He describes the problems and praises Hoggart's book as "a shrewd and careful essay."

3   COX, R.G. "Auden as Critic and Poet." Scrutiny, 18 (Autumn), 158-61.
    A generally negative view of Auden's The Enchafed Flood, which seems undisciplined, and of Hoggart's Auden (1951.A1), which though unpretentious seems vague and unconvincing.

4   DONAHUE, CHARLES. "Auden on Romanticism." Thought, 26 (Summer), 283-87.
    A review of The Enchafed Flood. Auden does not define Romanticism but "describes it in terms of its own symbols," the sea as an "escape from the desert." Auden provides a new humanism, more fleshy and less priggish, "tougher, broader, and more subtle than the old Boston variety...."

5   DOONE, RUPERT. "The Theatre of Ideas." Theatre Newsletter, 6 (29 September), 5.
    An account of the establishment, the aims, and the innovations of the Group Theatre in the early thirties. The Dance of Death was written for the group at Doone's request. Auden combined the idea of a ballet on the subject of Orpheus' descent and the idea of a play on the theme of le danse macabre.

6   FORSTER, E.M. "The Ascent of F.6," in Two Cheers for Democracy. New York: Harcourt, Brace, pp. 263-68.
    "The Ascent of F.6 is a tragedy in a modern mode, full of funniness and wisecracks." Forster describes the play

1951

by focusing the "heroic," the "politico-economic outlook,"
the individual character, and the Freudian view. He follows this brief commentary with another on The Enchafed
Flood (pp. 265-68). Auden rescues the sea from its retreat; he returns "Neptune his majesty." The book, however critical in tone, is a poem, which admonishes man to
rebuild the ruined city, the only course remaining to him.

7   KAVANAGH, PATRICK. "Auden and the Creative Mind." Envoy,
        5 (June), 33-39.
        Auden shares with all the great poets the quality called
    creativity. He does not teach nor philosophize; he is all
    delight and sensation. He has discovered "rich veins of
    gold" where we saw a bankrupt world. Auden's work, like
    that of all great writers, is without morality or didactic
    purpose, but is "an orgy of sensation."

8   ROTH, ROBERT. "The Sophistication of W.H. Auden: A Sketch in
        Longinian Method." Modern Philology, 48 (February), 193-
        204.
        Auden achieves Longinian "sublimity" without the "tra-
    ditional Longinian requisites of 'transport' and 'eleva-
    tion'" but rather by "a refusal to be carried away by the
    objects of his emotion, an overt skepticism of their
    loftiness--in short, a thoroughly modern temper of cool-
    ness and sophisticated reserve." Attempts to delineate
    the particular elements in Auden's work which Roth calls
    his "high seriousness."

9   SCOTT-JAMES, R.A. "Modern Poets," in his Fifty Years of
        English Literature 1900-1950. London: Longmans, pp.
        210-39.
        Auden is discussed as "the shining particular light"
    among a group of poets who are classified as in the
    "circle," on the "fringe, half in and half out," or out-
    side but influenced by the central poets of the group.
    The message of Auden's poetry is in his line, "O teach us
    to outgrow our madness." The other poets are compared to
    Auden. Brief comments on Nones and The Shield of Achilles
    appear in a second edition, 1956.B11.

10 SPEARS, MONROE K. "The Dominant Symbols of Auden's Poetry."
        Sewanee Review, 59 (July-September), 392-425.
        Six symbols appear significant "when Auden's work is
    studied as a whole": "War, the Quest, Paysage Logos, and
    the City." Describes each of these symbols and applies
    them to an analysis of The Age of Anxiety, which many
    critics have found "too artificial and rhetorical, lacking

in dramatic quality, ...unrealistic and superficial."
Spears answers those critics.

11   _____. "Late Auden: The Satirist as Lunatic Clergyman."
        Sewanee Review, 59 (January-March), 50-74.
            An analysis of Auden's poetry as the work of a satirist.
        Other critics have approached Auden from another aspect
        and have largely failed to notice that "his poetic strategy
        is more like that of Dryden and Pope than like that of
        Yeats or Eliot."

12   SPENDER, STEPHEN. "Seriously Unserious." Poetry, 78
        (September), 352-56.
            A review of Nones. Nones is influenced by Auden's
        living on the Island of Ischia, where he adopts ("a shot
        of") the Latin viewpoint. He gains or applies "a classical
        precision and detachment." Discusses Auden's style in
        general and in three poems "Memorial for the City,"
        "Prime," and "In Praise of Limestone."

13   _____. World Within World. New York: Harcourt, Brace,
        passim (esp. pp. 43-58).
            Autobiography of Spender, reactions to Auden, his
        personality and ideas. Recounts Spender's personal experi-
        ences with Auden, mostly at Oxford.

1952 A BOOKS

1   IZZO, CARLO. Poesie di W.H. Auden. Parma: Guanda.
            Translation with notes of selected poems by Auden; for
        Izzo's introduction, translated by Camilla Roatta, see
        1964.A4; 1964.B10.

1952 B SHORTER WRITINGS

1   ALLEN, WALTER. "W.H. Auden: 'The Most Exciting Living Poet.'"
        Listener, 47 (17 April), 640-41.
            Auden has had a strong influence on poetry and poets for
        twenty years. With his first book he caused the young
        poets writing then to scrap their verses and begin anew.
        Now, Allen finds him not best, but "most exciting." His
        faults hardly matter, "so great is the creative vigour of
        his writing." In his last poems (Nones) the light tone,
        which might be taken for weakness, is really strength; the
        voice is that of "a civilized man speaking to his equals."

1952

2   BRAYBROOKE, NEVILLE. "Auden: An Interim View." Books:
    The Journal of the National Book League, 275 (December),
    136-38.
        Despite the attempts of critics at writing off Auden
    "as a dead letter in contemporary literature," Auden con-
    tinues to bring forth "his best, most exciting and lyrical
    poetry" (Nones). Outlines and assesses Auden's poetic out-
    put to 1952.

3   DEUTSCH, BABETTE. "Science and Poetry," in her Poetry in Our
    Time. New York: Holt, 378-400.
        This discourse on modern poetry divides into two parts.
    The first discusses the characteristic viewpoint of Auden
    (who tried to be "clinically-minded"), reviewing his poems
    as illustrations of his intellectual curiosity. The sec-
    ond part turns to Auden's interest in music as well as
    other arts. He is compared with various poets like
    Shapiro, Eliot, Williams, Lowell, and others of the period.

4   ENRIGHT, D.J. "Reluctant Admiration: A Note on Auden and
    Rilke." Essays in Criticims, 2 (April), 180-95.
        Examines the effect of Rilke on Auden in respect to
    both strengths and weaknesses particularly in In Time of
    War and The Quest. From this influence Auden gains en-
    couragement of his "gift for the short, dramatic situa-
    tion," but his reaction to what might be called Rilke's
    "aestheticism" encourages instead "hardness, lack of
    sympathy, of faith in individuality, a further weakening
    in the sense of human dignity." Rilke might say of Auden
    that he "has been judging, instead of saying." And En-
    right concludes, "for all the signs of personal suffering
    which his poetry bears, perhaps he has often arrived too
    easily at his judgments." Reprinted: 1957.B4.

5   HOFFMAN, DANIEL G. "Auden's American Demigod," in Paul Bun-
    yan: Last of the Frontier Demigods. Philadelphia: Uni-
    versity of Pennsylvania Press for Temple University
    Publications, pp. 143-53.
        Discussion of Auden's operetta, its origins, plot,
    characterization, and versification. Auden worked under
    the handicaps of an unfamiliar form, a new kind of audience
    (High School) and limited knowledge of the character of
    Paul Bunyan. Hoffman thinks Auden could not make up his
    mind as to his intentions, for "the effect is so self-
    contradictory that no consistent direction gives the
    libretto dramatic force." Nevertheless, says Hoffman, it
    "lies in undeserved neglect"; it reveals Auden's "ambiva-
    lence toward America: half celebration, half disenchant-
    ment."

6 HUTCHINSON, PEARSE. "W.H. Auden: The Search for Happiness."
   Litterair Paspoort, 7 (October), 180-82.
      Only a great poet can write a successful poem about the
   search for happiness, and it is that achievement that
   makes Auden great. His outstanding merit is that he does
   not simplify but instead "admits the whole collection,
   with remorseless exactitude: disgust, desire, adoration,
   contempt...." Nones combines the two powerful "illusions"
   of love and religion.

7 MITCHELL, DONALD, AND HANS KELLER, eds. Benjamin Britten.
   London: Rockliff, passim.
      Beneficial influence of Auden on Britten's regard for
   poetry. Britten's music--the "cosmopolitan, European as-
   pect of Auden's poetry...appealed to Britten's imagination."
   Discusses generally the music of Britten rather than the
   poems of Auden. Hadrian's Wall, radio script by Auden,
   1938, scored by Britten, contains bibliographical items of
   Britten's incidental music based on or using Auden's work,
   pp. 311-13. Lists one recording of Auden's "Hymm to St.
   Cecilia," p. 355.

8 MOORE, GEOFFREY. "Three Who Did Not Make a Revolution."
   American Mercury, 74 (April), 107-14.
      Describes spiritual and social conditions to which
   Auden, Spender, and Isherwood reacted so as to seem com-
   munistic and revolutionary. Compares and contrasts Auden
   to Spender and Isherwood as to temperament and technique
   and lists the main publishing points of their careers. By
   moving to America, Moore thinks, Auden has traded one kind
   of difficulty for another, i.e., of "not being at home
   artistically." And of their bright revolutionary beginning, Moore says, "At all events it has become clear that
   there is no political panacea."

9 SAVAGE, HENRY. "Auden as Moralist." Poetry Review, 43
   (January-February), 24-29.
      Ostensibly a review of Hoggart's book, it contains in-
   formation and judgments on Auden resulting from disagree-
   ment with many of Hoggart's assertions as well as with
   many of Auden's. Savage believes that more of Hoggart's
   morality is in his book than Auden's, that "Mr. Auden
   himself might hardly subscribe to it." Auden's status as
   a poet ought to be the subject of criticism, and one of the
   problems in evaluating the poems is "whether art should or
   should not subserve morality."

1952

10 SHEPHERD, T.B. "'For the Time Being': W.H. Auden's Christ-
    mas Oratorio." London Quarterly & Holborn Review, 177
    (October), 277-84.
        Describes briefly Auden's "early period" of poems in a
    varied manner, earnest, conversational, even gossipy; even
    more briefly his didactic period, best expressed by his
    verse plays, showing Marxian and Freudian interests; and
    then at length the mature period of For the Time Being,
    pointing a change in direction. The anxiety marking the
    second period gives way to the exploration of religious
    belief. Then Love, treated in its numerous meanings in
    earlier verse, becomes "Christian love, which in turn
    needs description and examination."

11 WILDER, AMOS N. "Mr. W.H. Auden," in Modern Poetry and the
    Christian Tradition. New York: Scribners, pp. 196-204,
    251-56.
        Auden registers a "Protestant protest against false
    culture and false prophets" and presents "a positive faith
    and morality in Anglo-Catholic terms." He initiates "the
    religious spirit into...modern science, modern psychology,
    modern sociology, the modern sensibility and alienation."
    One theme of Auden's "Christmas Oratorio" is "that the
    initiation into estrangement and the exploration of the
    mistaken courses must proceed to their limit before the
    way out presents itself." Wilder concludes that although
    "ambiguous or heretical," productions like Auden's offer
    "Necessary criticism, correction and protest," and reveal
    roots "in our religious tradition...."

12 WILLIAMS, RAYMOND. "Auden and Isherwood," in his Drama from
    Ibsen to Eliot. London: Chatto & Windus, pp. 247-56.
        Revisions of the essay are mostly matters of wording,
    though the earlier version credits John Lehmann for some
    of the criticism. Examines The Dog Beneath the Skin, The
    Ascent of F-6, and On the Frontier as "examples of a lively
    and influential form of verse drama." Discusses the use
    of popular conventions like musical comedy and burlesque.
    He nevertheless concludes that Auden and Isherwood failed
    to achieve "any adequate dramatic integrity." Revised:
    1968.B18.

13 WILSON, EDMUND. "The Oxford Boys Becalmed," in The Shores
    of Light. New York: Farrar, Straus, pp. 669-73.
        After announcing his stand in his early works, Auden
    seems at a loss what to do next. Auden's language is
    energetic, his satire is brilliant and successful, and his
    rendering of the special ills of our society is unique;

but his voice is less personal in On This Island than
formerly, he seems to be imitating Housman, Yeats, and
Eliot, and his verse is not now distinguishable from that
of Louis MacNeice. Nevertheless, Auden and his group (all
around thirty years old) are "remarkable, at that age, in
having been able to say so well something that had not yet
been said at all."

1953 A   BOOKS - NONE

1953 B   SHORTER WRITINGS

1   BRAYBROOKS, NEVILLE.   "W.H. Auden: The Road from Marx,"
    America, 88 (21 March), 680-81.
        By Another Time (1940) "society has ceased to be a unit
    for Auden, and is only a collection of individuals, each
    isolated from the other."   But Auden incorporates his
    youthful ideas "into a maturer vision of the world."
    Moreover, Auden has "fused his angry social conscience
    with his rapidly growing religious conscience...."   Quotes
    a self-portrait written by Auden for Graham Greene's The
    Old School, 1934.

2   FRASER, G.S.   "The 1930s and the War Years," in his The
    Modern Writer and His World.   London: Derek Verschoyle,
    pp. 230-66.
        Auden is set against the backdrop of the time and of
    those who influenced him or were influenced by him.   His
    style is contrasted with the styles of Spender, Day Lewis,
    and MacNeice; and then Auden in turn becomes the poet with
    whom still others are compared (e.g. Bottrall and Empson).

3   KALLMAN, CHESTER.   "New Stravinsky Opera: 'The Rake's
    Progress' to Have Its American Premiere on Saturday."
    New York Herald Tribune (8 February), sect. 4, p. 6.
        An account of some of the necessary considerations in
    writing the libretto for "The Rake's Progress."   Auden and
    Kallman had to create arias, for example, that would re-
    veal a character immediately, in contrast to a dramatist
    who could disclose very gradually a character's state of
    being.

4   SPENDER, STEPHEN.   "The Theme of Political Orthodoxy in the
    'Thirties,'" in The Creative Element: A Study of Vision,
    Despair, and Orthodoxy Among Some Modern Writers.   London:
    Hamish Hamilton, pp. 140-58.

1953

Auden's "poems have an almost chameleon-like quality of taking on the colour of the time in which they were written," and thus they reflect the "stages of development from the 1920's to the 1930's." Surveys from book to book Auden's development, for example, "from the style of his earliest poetry to the technical virtuosity and the dogmatic themes" of his later poems. It relates to <u>orthodoxy</u> "because no writer intelligently aware of the situation could imagine himself to be standing outside the society which produced unemployment and concentration camps." Thus "works of individual vision" are not possible.

5   ____. "W.H. Auden and His Poetry." <u>Atlantic</u>, 192 (July), 74-79.
       Contains biographical details and comments on Auden's personality. Argues that Auden's work is "depersonalized," that he is "outside" his poetry in ways that Eliot or Yeats or Thomas is not. "We feel that the poet has arrived at...conclusions by a process of reasoning which is outside the reasoning of his blood." Reprinted: 1964.A3.

1954 A BOOKS - NONE

1954 B SHORTER WRITINGS

1   ANEY, EDITH T. "British Poetry of Social Protest in the 1930's: The Problem of Belief in the Poetry of W.H. Auden, C. Day Lewis, 'Hugh MacDiarmid,' Louis MacNeice, and Stephen Spender." Ph.D. dissertation, University of Pennsylvania.
       In the general revolt by the poets of social protest against representatives of authority and "the middle class," Auden's uncompromising belief in the ideals of truth and love enabled him to produce a "poetry of an enduring quality" in contrast to those who wrote merely propaganda. Abstracted in <u>Dissertation Abstracts</u>, 14, 11 (1954), 2061.

2   DUNCAN, CHESTER. "The Compassion of W.H. Auden." <u>Canadian Forum</u>, 34 (April), 12-13.
       The reputation of Auden's poetry as difficult and obscure serves merely as an excuse for not reading it; it would, in fact, disarm many critics with its "lyrical intensity and charm of manner" if they were less "determined to be difficult." Attributed to Auden is the "renewal of the compassionate tradition." He is more direct and less ambiguous than Eliot in his treatment of humane feelings in verse.

3 KERMAN, JOSEPH. "Opera a la Mode." Hudson Review, 6
   (Winter), 560-77.
       Points out weaknesses in both conception and execution
   in The Rake's Progress, but also replies to objections
   made by other critics. Describes the music and the plot,
   making appreciative comments, and after high praise returns
   to the chief fault, the unarticulated conclusion of the
   opera. Reprinted: 1954.B4. Revised: 1956.B8.

4 _____. "Opera a la Mode." Opera (London), 5 (July),
   411-15.
       Reprint of 1954.B3.

5 SEIF, MORTON. "The Impact of T.S. Eliot on Auden and
   Spender." South Atlantic Quarterly, 53 (January), 61-69.
       As members of the generation succeeding Eliot, Auden
   and Spender receive the deepest influence. Discusses this
   influence on Auden's sensibility, thought, language, and
   technique, and also on his experiemnts in verse drama.
   Attempts some one to one correspondences in the two poets.

6 SOUTHWORTH, J.G. "W.H. Auden: 1940 and After," in his More
   Modern American Poets. London: Oxford University Press,
   pp. 120-36.
       Evaluates Auden's output, 1940-1951, Another Time to
   Nones. Finds the same subjects as earlier but with new
   emphases. Auden has a deeper understanding of the causes
   of the ills of society he had noted in his earlier works
   (i.e., economic man's pursuit of profit). His technique
   has matured, but now he has a "harder surface" and
   "reaches the heights" less frequently. Auden's light
   verse "is the finest we have today."

7 WEISGERBER, JEAN. "W.H. Auden as Critic (1930-1941)."
   Revue des Langues Vivantes, 20, No. 2, 116-25.
       Places Auden's poetry in the stream of English social
   criticism. Auden's criticism falls into three parts; not
   necessarily chronological, they are "successively...
   capitalism, dictatorship, and the human condition." For
   about ten years Auden concerns himself with the deficien-
   cies of capitalism, during which time he turns sincerely
   if "superficially" to communism. Hitler's rise to power
   prompts Auden to become "the mouthpiece of anti-Fascism,"
   although his hatred of war is stronger than his hatred of
   Fascism. "On the eve of the war, he gives up the struggle" and comes to the United States; his belief in the
   need for forgiveness and confession and "his need of iso-
   lation" make him withdraw from action.

1954

8   WINGATE, GIFFORD W. "Poetic Drama in the 1930's: A Study of
        the Plays of T.S. Eliot and W.H. Auden." Ph.D. disserta-
        tion, Cornell University.
            Evaluates the success of Auden and Eliot in relating the
        forms of poetry and drama. Studies the formal elements as
        dictated by the authors' attitudes and intentions and con-
        cludes that both failed "to define the positive values
        within their respective dramatic context."

1955 A BOOKS - NONE

1955 B SHORTER WRITINGS

1   CLANCY, JOSEPH. "A W.H. Auden Bibliography 1924-1955."
        Thought, 30 (Summer), 260-70.
            Lists (with very few misprints) Auden's books under
        headings of Poems, Dramatic Works, and Prose; his Uncol-
        lected Materials, including Juvenilia, Essays and Reviews,
        introductions to Books, and three Miscellaneous items
        (musical pieces; ninety-seven articles and books about
        Auden; and Recordings of Auden's readings). A number of
        the items about Auden are negative reviews, most of which
        do not appear in Bloomfield and Mendelson (1972.A2).

2   GRAVES, ROBERT. "These Be Your Gods, O Israel!" Essays in
        Criticism, 5 (April), 145-47.
            Finds Auden derivative, even to the point of borrowing
        half lines from Laura Riding; and, as the title hints,
        sees any regard for Auden as "idolatry." Reprinted:
        1955.B3; 1956.B6; 1956.B7.

3   _____. "These Be Your Gods, O Isreal!" in his The Crowning
        Privilege. London: Cassell, pp. 130-32.
            Reprint of 1955.B2.

4   GREENWOOD, ORMEROD. "It Was Something Like This...." Ark
        (London), 15: 35-38.
            An account of the early struggles of the Group Theatre
        (London) and briefly of Auden's connection with it.

5   KNOLL, ROBERT E. "The Style of Contemporary Poetry."
        Prairie Schooner, 29 (Summer), 118-25.
            Auden's sonnet "The Diaspora" requires readers to
        examine its details closely and rewards them for doing so.
        The change in title from "The Jew Wrecked in the German
        Cell" suggests a broader application; the essay discusses
        some of the ramifications and compares the poem to a

sonnet by Wordsworth. The discussion all relates to dif-
ferences between the Romantic style and the modern style.

6   LEHMANN, JOHN. The Whispering Gallery. London: Longmans,
    Green, passim.
       Recounts various experiences with Auden and an opinion
    of Auden's personality, behavior, and works. Some pas-
    sages merely mention Auden; index is useful for isolating
    particular comments. I Am My Brother (1960.B10) repeats
    most of the anecdotes and references and has almost no
    new material on Auden. The third book In My Own Time
    (1969.B8) reprints these two books. Reprinted: 1960.B10;
    1969.B8.

7   MacFADDEN, GEORGE. "The Rake's Progress: A Note on the
    Libretto." Hudson Review, 8 (Spring), 105-12.
       Since Auden has created a fable in The Rake's Progress,
    critics should so read it. Compares Auden's intentions
    with Hogarth's and discusses the differences in treatment
    of characters. Defends Auden's Epilogue against the
    criticisms of Kerman (1954.B3).

8   MOORE, MARIANNE. "W.H. Auden," in her Predilections. New
    York: Viking Press, pp. 84-102.
       Quotes liberally from Auden's verse and prose, showing
    the nature of his themes and ideas and, of course, his
    personality. Our debt to Auden is for the emphasis he
    has placed on free will and moral responsibility.

9   SPENDER, STEPHEN. "It Began at Oxford." New York Times
    (13 March), sect. 7, pp. 4-5.
       Although the "Oxford group" was an invention by others
    (the members never met as a group or talked of themselves
    as a movement), Spender, Day Lewis, MacNeice, and Auden
    had much in common. Lists these common traits and gives
    some account of their divergent ways; confesses that they,
    too, came to accept the "myth of a coherent movement"; and
    concludes that perhaps what they did have in common was
    "Oxford, after all."

10 STEINBERG, ERWIN R. "Poetic Drama in General and Auden and
    Isherwood in Particular." Carnegie Studies in English, 2:
    43-58.
       Poetry in The Dog Beneath the Skin is reserved for the
    chorus, the rest is prose and doggerel. Poetry will bear
    more images than prose and thus allows swifter movement
    than prose and "provides economy and efficiency." The
    serious poetry of the chorus contrasts with the doggerel

1955

and bestows "dignity" on "the criticism leveled at society...." The Ascent of F6 similarly employs its verse but in addition uses it at times of "great emotional intensity." The best poetry is reserved for Michael Ransom, the hero.

11   WEALES, GERALD. "A Little Faith, a Little Envy: A Note on Santayana and Auden." American Scholar, 24 (Summer), 340-47.
      Auden's resentment of Santayana as expressed in his review for the New Yorker, May 2, 1953, lies in an unwillingness to accept the terms of Santayana's dogma, although it is the very dogma Auden seeks. Compares the different personalities of Auden and Santayana, noting what the tone of Auden's comments reveals about himself. Auden is apparently annoyed by Santayana's intellectual self-sufficiency and certainty.

1956 A   BOOKS - NONE

1956 B   SHORTER WRITINGS

1   ANON. "The Dog Beneath the Gown." New Statesman and Nation, 51 (9 June), 656-57.
      Auden is not "representative" as has often been said but "different from most people." Everything for him is a matter of conscious choice; and he chooses "as one who distrusts the intellect," although he is intelligent. Moreover, he likes to shock, to mystify and elaborate. Following such assertions is a review of Auden's career from birth to his election as Oxford Professor of Poetry. Reprinted: 1957.B1.

2   ANON. "Profile of a Poet." Observer (9 December), p. 5.
      A look at Auden as "inky fag" with "a fag's oddity and freshness." A brief biographical outline of Auden from school at Gresham's Holt, at Oxford, and then abroad in Weimar, Germany, Abyssinia, Spain, and Manchuria. Auden is politically naive, never having made a serious study of politics; his departure to America "was an excited desire to explore a new continent and an unknown civilisation." Finally, the writer comments on Auden's appointment to the professorship of poetry at Oxford as "a surprising but an excellent appointment."

3   ANSEN, ALAN. "A Communication." Hudson Review, 9 (Summer), 319-20.

W. H. Auden: A Reference Guide

1956

A reply to McFadden's article (1955.B7), which Ansen thinks unscholarly in ignoring Kallman's contributions to the text of The Rake's Progress. Consequently, praise for lines quoted by McFadden "redound...to the credit of Mr. Kallman...." Apportions the responsibility for particular scenes between the authors.

4 BENNETT, DAPHNE NICHOLSON. "Auden's 'September 1, 1939': An Interpreter's Analysis." Quarterly Journal of Speech, 42 (February), 1-13.
    Attempts to apply principles of literary criticism to the problems of the oral interpreter. Sets Auden's poem "September 1, 1939" first in its historical period, then examines its "viewpoint," and finally its metrics as a concern of the oral interpreter for placing emphasis.

5 FRASER, G.S. "The Young Prophet." New Statesman and Nation, 51 (28 January), 102-103.
    The notable quality of The Orators is energy, and that energy carried readers of the thirties over many obscure or mysterious parts, since generally it seemed clear. Then readers took the implied politics as Marxist, for Auden described himself as "pink liberal"; but now the politics seem those of a "romantic radical of the Right." The book "stirred the consciences of intelligent young men in a bad time," and that is what a prophet should do. Reprinted: 1959.B4; 1960.B6.

6 GRAVES, ROBERT. "These Be Your Gods, O Israel!" in his The Crowning Privilege. New York: Doubleday, pp. 136-38.
    American edition of 1955.B3.

7 _____. "These Be Your Gods, O Isreal!" New Republic, 124 (5 March), 17-18.
    Reprint of 1955.B2.

*8 KERMAN, JOSEPH. "Opera a la Mode," in his Opera as Drama. New York: Knopf, pp. 234-49.
    Revised version of 1954.B3 and B4. Not seen. Cited in 1972.A2.

9 MARTIN, W.B.J. "W.H. Auden and the Preacher." Congregational Quarterly, 34 (October), 354-60.
    First chides the preachers for ignoring modern poets and then illustrates their loss by recounting the values of reading Auden; for Auden is not just a Christian poet but something rarer, a Protestant poet. Auden's clearest treatment of his Protestantism may be found in "For the

45

1956

Time Being"; and in the scenes between the Wise Men and the
Shepherds, Auden proves he has grasped both "the modern
predicament and...the Christian answer."

10   REPLOGLE, JUSTIN M. "The Auden Group: The 1930's Poetry of
W.H. Auden, C. Day Lewis, and Stephen Spender." Ph.D.
dissertation, University of Wisconsin.
Auden's response to the social problems of the thirties
was to try to attract a wide audience by writing in the
forms of "burlesque, buffoonery, comic satire, and a number of other verse techniques not capable of brief classi-
fication." Also treats the reactions of other poets in the
group. Abstracted in Dissertation Abstracts, 17, 11, 2169.

11   SCOTT-JAMES, R.A. "Postscript 1951-1955," in his Fifty Years
of English Literature 1900-1950. Second edition. London:
Longmans, pp. 251-52.
Adds brief comments on Nones and The Shield of Achilles
to update views expressed in the earlier edition. Second
edition of 1951.B9.

12   THOMPSON, JOHN. "Auden at the Sheldonian." Truth, 156 (15
June), 690.
Personal, "human" account of Auden's lecture as 33rd
Professor of Poetry, "the first alien ever to hold that
high office," describing Auden, his lecture, and the au-
dience.

13   WILSON, EDMUND. "W.H. Auden in America." New Statesman and
Nation, 51 (9 June), 658-59.
The influence of America has not "diluted in the least
the Englishness" of Auden, which is an Englishness now out
of style in the literary world. Rather, America has helped
him "acquire...a mind that feels itself at the center of
things...a point of view that is inter- or super-national."
Auden with ease and naturalness appropriated American
speech, customs, and allusions for his verse. Although
he is one of the most technically accomplished poets, he
is also "one of the most edible, one of the most satis-
factory...."; Collected Poetry, for example, sold over
thirty thousand copies. Reprinted 1964.A4.

1957 A BOOKS

1   BEACH, JOSEPH WARREN. The Making of the Auden Canon.
Minneapolis: University of Minnesota Press.

A record of revisions in Auden's Collected Poetry (1945)
and Collected Shorter Poems (1950) along with Beach's comments and speculations about the motives for the changes.
Concludes that the "probable" reasons are "about equally
divided between considerations of artistry and considerations having to do with his political, social, and religious philosophy" and not infrequently to both reasons.
"Supplementary Notes" adds instances of "minor retouchings"
for those "interested in poetic craftsmanship." Contains
a brief bibliography and an index of Auden's poems and the
volumes containing the poems referred to in the main text.

2   HOGGART, RICHARD. W.H. Auden. Writers and Their Work, No.
     93. London: Longmans for the British Council.
        A general introduction to Auden. Relates the man to
     his works through his themes and techniques and attempts
     to delineate his personality and his intellectual develop-
     ment. Divides Auden's work into "1930 to the War Years,"
     "From the 'Forties to the Mid-'fifties," and "In the Mean-
     time." Updated with revised bibliography by J.W. Robinson
     1965.B15. Reprinted text only: 1970.B11.

3   ROWAN, MARK. "Politics in the Early Poetry of W.H. Auden,
     1930-1945." Ph.D. dissertation, Cornell University.
        Because critics saw Auden's poetry in the thirties as
     Marxist, they saw his forties' poems, which stressed
     "man's relation to God," as a conversion. These poems,
     however, continue Auden's concern for justice achieved
     through love and do not mark a repudiation of former be-
     liefs as implied by the term "conversion." Abstracted in
     Dissertation Abstracts, 17 (December), 3023-24.

1957 B   SHORTER WRITINGS

1   ANON. "The Dog Beneath the Gown," in New Statesman Profiles.
     London: Phoenix House, pp. 211-16.
        Reprint of 1956.B1.

2   BAYLEY, JOHN. "W.H. Auden," in The Romantic Survival; A
     Study in Poetic Evolution. London: Constable, pp. 127-
     85.
        Auden's poetry teaches us how to live in the actual
     world by stressing that art is one thing and life another.
     He implies thereby that the poet is separate from the man.
     The poet may "indulge in all the romantic attitudes: the
     man must conform to the classical moral pattern." Com-
     pares Auden to Yeats and Eliot as a means of focusing
     what is distinctively Auden, who has created a myth from

1957

the details of actual life. Ranges over the corpus of
Auden's work, but treats principally Poems (1930). Ex-
cerpts reprinted: 1964.A4.

3   BREWER, D.S. "Dualism in the Poetry of W.H. Auden." Eigo
     Eibungaku Kenkyu (Hiroshima), 4 (July), 1-14.
          Applies the thesis that Auden attempts to reconcile the
     irreconcilable to several poems in The Shield of Achilles.
     Considers obvious kinds of duality like new and old and
     less obvious kinds like Arcadia and Utopia. Auden suggests
     that opposites "complete each other," resolving "the duality
     of experience, by accepting it, and by going beyond it...."

4   ENRIGHT, D.J. "Reluctant Admiration: A Note on Auden and
     Rilke," in his The Apothecary's Shop: Essays on Litera-
     ture. London: Secker & Warburg, pp. 187-205.
          Reprint of 1952.B4.

5   HYAMS, C. BARRY, AND KARL H. REICHERT. "A Test Lesson on
     Brueghel's 'Icarus' and Auden's 'Musee des Beaux Arts.'"
     Die Neueren Sprachen, n.s. 6 (May), 228-32.
          A discussion of the painting and the poem in the form
     of a lesson plan: questions by a Teacher, answers by a
     Pupil. Teacher and pupil scrutinize both in detail for
     the purpose of interpretation.

6   KERMAN, JOSEPH. "Auden's 'Magic Flute.'" Hudson Review, 10
     (Summer), 309-16.
          Kallman and Auden acted boldly in making their transla-
     tion of Die Zauberflote also an interpretation and managed
     to achieve a "tone of quiet elegance" and to solve several
     difficult problems. Their change of Mozart's plot, how-
     ever, sacrifices the "human theme" to the "metaphysical
     theme" and "militates against the practical use" of this
     translation. A comparison of the translation with "The
     Sea and the Mirror" explains the liberties Auden has
     taken with Mozart's work.

7   KOCH, KENNETH. "New Books by Marianne Moore and W.H. Auden."
     Poetry, 90 (April), 47-52.
          Auden is disappointing in the seven poems of The Old
     Man's Road; he is too flat and abstract. The poems are
     stale imitations of themes Auden has more skillfully
     handled and now "seem like intellectual exercises."

8   McALEER, EDWARD C. "As Auden Walked Out." College English,
     18 (February), 271-72.

Auden stays within the convention of romantic balla-
deering for five stanzas of "As I Walked Out One Evening,"
until he injects the message of the clocks "that love does
not last."

9   MOORE, GERALD. "Luck in Auden." Essays in Criticism, 7
     (January), 103-108.
          The word luck is a favorite with Auden and also names
     an important concept. Listed and explicated are numerous
     uses Auden makes of the word, all pointing to a concept of
     luck relating to Auden's concept of love. Consequently,
     luck gives way to love in the later poems.

10   THWAITE, ANTHONY. "W.H. Auden," in his Essays on Contemporary
     English Poetry. Tokyo: Kenkyusha, pp. 65-81.
          Notwithstanding the criticism of Auden as essentially a
     practitioner of light verse or as really "two Audens,"
     either "the left-wing intellectual" or "the Christian
     intellectual," Thwaite finds "a wholeness...rather than a
     division" even in Auden's injection of lightness of tone
     into his serious poems. The tone "is not one of triviality,
     but of the surgeon who...makes a wry joke as he goes into
     the operating theatre." Examines the meaning of the word
     love in Auden's poetry and decides that Auden shows how
     impossible and absurd it is to be dogmatic about love.
     Reprinted: 1959.B8.

11   WHITTEMORE, REED. "Auden on Americans." Sewanee Review, 65
     (Winter), 145-51.
          Challenges Auden's assertion that colleges should not
     teach courses in modern literature and argues that Auden
     in editing an anthology (The Criterion Book of Modern
     American Verse, 1956) and writing an introduction for it is
     teaching like any college professor. Auden's selections
     all illustrate his thesis of "(a) American fingering, (b)
     American independence from Western culture, and (c)
     American preoccupation with big pictures and underlying
     motives." Selections for each poet are too few to be
     representative and odd besides, i.e., unfamiliar, so as
     to make the anthology "a refuge for readers...tired of
     'Stopping by Woods.'"

1958 A BOOKS

1   CALLAN, EDWARD. An Annotated Checklist of the Works of
     W.H. Auden (1924-1957). Denver: Alan Swallow, 26 pp.
          Limited edition of 1958.B2.

1958

1958 B   SHORTER WRITINGS

1   ALVAREZ, A.   "W.H. Auden: Poetry and Journalism," in The
    Shaping Spirit: Studies in Modern English and American
    Poets. London: Chatto & Windus, pp. 87-106.
        Compared to other modern poets like Yeats, Eliot or
    Stevens, Auden produces work that is "peripheral, a poetry
    of technique, brilliant critical insights and ingenuity."
    Auden has two writers in him, the poet and the hack; the
    journalist in him treats externals and surfaces, not "their
    real nature." American title of this book is Stewards of
    Excellence (New York: Scribners, 1958).

2   CALLAN, EDWARD.   "An Annotated Checklist of the Works of
    W.H. Auden (1924-1957)." Twentieth Century Literature,
    4 (April-July), 30-50.
        Lists volumes of Auden's poetry, not the publications
    of individual poems. Gives descriptive annotations also
    of Auden's critical and expository prose. Has 307 items.
    Reprinted in a limited edition: 1958.A1; continued
    1970.B4. Also included in 1959.A1.

3   _____.   "The Development of W.H. Auden's Poetic Theory
    Since 1940." Twentieth Century Literature, 4 (October),
    79-91.
        Auden's critical writings often treat themes appearing
    in his poetry and thus supply information about "the view
    of life and the theory of art from which his poetry
    stems." Early his concern had been with metaphysics, and
    in the forties Kierkegaard assumes prime significance in
    Auden's aesthetic theory. He accepts Kierkegaard's
    categories of modes of awareness and believes each cate-
    gory implies a different form of artistic expression; he
    then synthesizes what he thinks to be the best insights
    of Freud and Marx with Kierkegaard's.

4   GERSTENBERGER, DONNA L.   "Formal Experiments in Modern Verse
    Drama." Ph.D. dissertation, University of Oklahoma.
        Discusses the point of view and techniques used by
    Auden (and others) to "revitalize" verse drama for modern
    audiences. Abstracted in Dissertation Abstracts, 19
    (January 1959), 1757-58.

5   NELSON, HUGH A.   "Individuals of a Group: The 1930's Poetry
    of W.H. Auden, C. Day Lewis and Stephen Spender." Ph.D.
    dissertation, Northwestern University.
        Studies the characteristics that make the Auden Group
    a group and then emphasizes the differences, especially in

individual political beliefs. Finds Auden's language more
expressive of "a commitment to political action than he ac-
tually felt." It is this language, along with metaphors
from science and psychology, that accounts for his "clin-
ical detachment." Abstracted in Dissertation Abstracts,
19 (December 1958), 1389-A.

6   RODWAY, A.E. AND F.W. COOK. "An Altered Auden." Essays in
     Criticism, 8 (July), 303-19.
         Reviews Beach's The Making of the Auden Canon, dis-
     cusses some of the changes in Auden's poems listed there,
     and offers interpretations of the poems as affected by
     Auden's alterations. Many poems are discussed briefly,
     two at some length, "A Summer Night 1933" and "Through
     the Looking Glass."

1959 A   BOOKS

1   CALLAN, EDWARD T. O'DWYER. "A Study of the Relationship of
     Structure and Meaning in W.H. Auden's Major Poems, 1940-
     1955; Together with an Annotated Checklist of W.H. Auden's
     Published Writings, 1924-1957." D.Litt. dissertation,
     University of South Africa.
         The "Annotated Checklist" is the same as 1958.B2.
     Applies Auden's aesthetic theory to his poems, particularly
     "New Year Letter,"The Sea and the Mirror," "For the Time
     Being," and "The Age of Anxiety," Auden's poems are best
     approached "through their structure."

1959 B   SHORTER WRITINGS

1   BLOOMFIELD, B.C. "Notes and Corrections on 'The Making of
     the Auden Canon,' by J.W. Beach." Notes and Queries, n.s.
     6 (June), 227-28.
         Lists twenty-two additions or corrections to Beach's
     book (1957.A1), supplying information about printings, re-
     printings, and misprintings of Auden's works.

2   CLANCY, JOSEPH P. "Auden Waiting for his City." Christian
     Scholar, 42 (Fall), 185-200.
         Auden's attempt to make the City an image of the "com-
     plexity of human values" is the most sustained of modern
     poets. Traces the growth of this image chronologically
     in Auden's poems from the City as "symbol of social dis-
     order and decay" to "man's final goal outside time."

1959

3   DONOGHUE, DENIS. "Drame a These: Auden and Cummings," in
     The Third Voice. Princeton: Princeton University Press,
     pp. 62-29.
         The weaknesses of The Ascent of F6 are first pointed
     out and discussed and then later the strengths of Cumming's
     Santa Claus to form a contrast. The Ascent of F6 dilutes
     Eliot's "style" into a "manner," is uncertain in tone and
     poise, is "crudely organised," and is "more interested in
     these than in drame."

4   FRASER, G.S. Vision and Rhetoric. London: Fabor, pp. 149-
     78.
         Three chapters take up Auden's career from Fraser's
     personal point of view: his own changing attitudes about
     Auden, his quarrel with Auden's ideas, his doubtful ad-
     miration for Auden. The articles are, however, critical
     of the poetry, not of Auden's career in a biographical
     sense. Reprints 1956.B5; reprinted 1960.B6; excerpts as
     "The Career of W.H. Auden" in 1964.A4.

5   MARTIN, W.B.J. "Significant Modern Writers: W.H. Auden."
     Expository Times, 71 (November), 36-38.
         Auden came to Christianity only after exploring other
     paths, having been guided by his experience in the Spanish
     Civil War, acquaintance with Charles Williams, and "a
     viewing of the Nazi film, Sieg im Poland. Explores the
     nature of Auden's faith (he is no dogmatist) and accounts
     for critical attacks on him (a result of his faith).
     Auden "has documented with clinical realism" man's need
     for love.

6   SCOTT, NATHAN A. "The Poetry of Auden." Chicago Review, 22
     (Winter), 53-75.
         Enumerates some of the negative criticisms of Auden's
     work, forming a capsule history of the unfavorable atti-
     tudes towards Auden, and answers them point by point. He
     advises those who wish to understand Auden to read New
     Year Letter, "his greatest poem." Attempts to define the
     nature of Auden's "vision." Reprinted: 1961.B12; re-
     vised and shortened 1965.B24.

7   SUNESEN, BENT. "'All We Are Stares Back at What We Are':
     A Note on Auden." English Studies, 40: 439-49.
         Suggests that The Sea and the Mirror bears an important
     relation to the rest of Auden's works. For Auden has
     always sought the nature and meaning of myth and attempted
     to justify the poet "as a creator of unifying, curative
     myth." All of Auden's habits and idiosyncracies relate to
     his "mythopoeic tendency."

8   THWAITE, ANTHONY. "W.H. Auden," in his Contemporary English
        Poetry. London: Heinemann, pp. 65-78.
            Reprint of 1957.B10.

1960 A BOOKS

1   BAHLKE, GEORGE W. "The Poetry of W.H. Auden: 1941-1955."
        Ph.D. Dissertation, Yale University.
            Places chief emphasis on works since 1939, Auden's
        "second major phase." Studies the influence of Auden's
        reading of Kierkegaard, Tillich, Niebuhr, and C. Williams
        on his decision to emigrate and as it is expressed in his
        writing. Offers a close reading of Auden's long poems,
        their themes and relationship to other poems. Auden's
        work has a good kind of didacticism, "it directs man toward
        knowledge of himself." Somewhat revised parts appear in
        1970.A1.

1960 B SHORTER WRITINGS

1   BEACH, JOSEPH WARREN. Obsessive Images. Minneapolis:
        University of Minnesota, pp. 104-13, passim.
            Auden among many other poets illustrates Beach's sub-
        ject as expressed in the subtitle "Symbolism in Poetry of
        1930's and 1940's." Scattered references to Auden appear
        throughout (readers should use the index); "Paysage
        Moralise" supplies a key symbol for Beach and forms an
        important aspect of his discussion. Auden has created
        numerous images adopted by the poets of the period.

2   BROOKS, CLEANTH, AND R.P. WARREN. "As I Walked Out One
        Evening," in their Understanding Poetry. Third edition.
        New York: Hold, Rinehart & Winston, pp. 330-35. Not in
        earlier editions.
            Auden's poem "As I Walked Out One Evening" uses con-
        ventions of the ballad and of Tin Pan Alley. Auden care-
        fully arranges the imagery of the first part to prepare
        for the later imagery.

3   CHARNEY, MAURICE. "Sir Lewis Namier and Auden's 'Musee des
        Beaux Arts.'" Philological Quarterly, 39 (January), 129-
        31.
            A passage in Namier's England in the Age of the Ameri-
        can Revolution (1930) parallels the point of view and the
        idea expressed by Auden in his poem. Both portray Brue-
        ghel's Icarus as an illustration of ironic humor.

1960

4   COOK, F.W.   "The Wise Fool: W.H. Auden and the Management."
     Twentieth Century, 168 (September), 219-27.
          Auden's interpretation of the Fool in King Lear implies
     a parallel between the role of poet and the role of Fool.
     Analyzes the later poems from this viewpoint, touching on
     Auden's increasing frivolity and playfulness.

5   DAY LEWIS, C.   The Buried Day.   New York: Harper & Row,
     passim.
          Personal reminiscence of Auden at Oxford and later: on
     his appearance, personality, and intelligence.   No index;
     see pp. 25, 176-79, 185-86, 216-17.

6   FRASER, G.S.   Vision and Rhetoric.   New York: Barnes & Noble,
     pp. 149-55.
          Reprint of 1959.B4.

7   HIGHET, GILBERT.   "Auden on the Baby: Kicking His Mother,"
     in The Powers of Poetry.   New York: Oxford University
     Press, pp. 167-73.
          "Mundus et Infans" has double and triple meanings "be-
     cause a baby is full of double and triple meanings."
     Auden regretfully admires the baby, as revealed in the
     ambiguity of the first line.

8   LARKIN, PHILIP.   "What's Become of Wystan?"   Spectator (15
     July), pp. 104-5.
          Believes Auden "no longer touches our imaginations."

9   LEAVIS, F.R.   "Retrospect 1950," in his New Bearings in
     English Poetry.   Ann Arbor: University of Michigan Press,
     pp. 215-38.
          Comments on Auden and other poets.

10   LEHMANN, JOHN.   I Am My Brother.   London: Longmans, Green,
     passim.
          Repeats most of the material about Auden in the earlier
     book The Whispering Gallery and adds very little new ma-
     terial.   See 1955.B6.

11   LERNER, LAURENCE.   "The Truest Poetry is the Most Feigning,"
     in The Truest Poetry.   London: Hamish Hamilton, pp. 204-7.
          Auden reconciles the apparent paradoxes of poetry as a
     game and poetry as a serious search for truth by arguing
     that unless a poet likes "hanging around words" instead
     of thinking he has important statements to make he will
     not "tap the fountain."

12   MAES-JELINEK, HENA. "The Knowledge of Man in the Works of
     Christopher Isherwood." Revue des Langues Vivantes, 26,
     No. 5, 341-60.
        Auden's plays in collaboration with Isherwood express
     attitudes the authors held at that time. The Dog Beneath
     the Skin and On the Frontier are social and political in
     theme and "were meant to stir the public conscience...."
     They focus on problems, not on characters. The Ascent of
     F6, however, presents an individual faced with "the claims"
     of his own nature and those made on him by society. A
     minor aspect overshadows the main problem ("Ransom's ex-
     cessive love for his mother"), which is then by-passed.
     The authors focus "the dangers of power, even when wielded
     by an enlightened man." Describes briefly the reactions
     to Auden's and Isherwood's emigration to the United States.
     Except for pp. 348-51 the article is about Isherwood.

13   MUSTE, JOHN M. "The Spanish Civil War in the Literature of
     the United States and Great Britain." Ph.D. dissertation,
     University of Wisconsin.
        Includes Auden briefly among numerous writers disil-
     lusioned by the failure of Marxian ideology in the Spanish
     Civil War. See pp. 149-55. Abstracted in Dissertation
     Abstracts, 21 (December 1960), 1568-69.

14   PEEL, MARIE. "Modern Poets: W.H. Auden." Writing Today, 10
     (December), 7-8.
        Surveys Auden's career, commenting on his subjects,
     themes, manner, and faith; finds the poetry of the fifties
     more reflective ("a kind of verse essay") but less exciting
     than the earlier poems.

15   PUDNEY, JOHN. "Auden As Schoolboy." Guardian, (21 May),
     p. 6.
     Excerpts from 1960.B16.

16   _____. Home and Away. London: Michael Joseph, pp. 45-
     49, 97-98, 206.
        Personal reminiscence of Auden at Gresham, of Auden and
     Britten at work on "Roman Wall Blues" for a BBC broadcast,
     and about Auden's correspondence with the author. Relates
     anecdotes about Auden's personality and actions. One
     morning Auden threw all his poems into a pond, returning
     later that night to retrieve them. "Thus the works that
     eventually came under the eye of T.S. Eliot at Fabers...
     were prudently salvaged from aqueous oblivion." Excerpt
     reprinted: 1960.B15.

1960

17   QUINN, SISTER M. BERNETTA, O.S.F. "Auden's City of God."
      Four Quarters, 9 (March), 5–8.
           A dominant symbol in Auden is the Just City, which may
      be examined in four senses: the literal, the allegorical,
      the tropological, and the anagogical. Reviews Auden's
      assertions about the difficulties of achieving the "Au-
      thentic City" and the dangers of building a false one,
      "Metropolis" or the "Unjust City."

18   _____. "Persons and Places in Auden." Renascence, 12
      (Spring), 115–24, 148.
           Auden uses both particular persons and places to repre-
      sent the universal human condition. Spells out in detail
      Auden's perspective through his private inner landscape,
      his childhood regions, England, Spain, the Just City, and
      the individuals there as "isomorphs" of us all.

19   REPLOGLE, JUSTIN. "Social Philosophy in Auden's Early
      Poetry." Criticism, 2 (Fall), 351–61.
           Traces the changes in Auden's views from the "psycho-
      logical" stage through the "Marxist" stage to the "Chris-
      tian" stage. The essay concerns itself principally with
      the early stage and the nature of Auden's "social philo-
      sophy" before 1935.

20   ROSENTHAL, M.L. "New Heaven and Earth--Auden and the
      'Thirties," in The Modern Poets. New York: Oxford
      University Press, pp. 182–96.
           There is always something "unfinished," or "occasional,"
      about Auden's poems that makes him a lesser poet than, for
      example, W.B. Yeats. The clue, however, to Auden's
      "relevancy" has been the questions he asks, not his ans-
      wers; he asks about revolution, uncertainties, ethical
      commitment. They reveal a sensibility eager "to find for
      itself a new birth in a new heaven and earth."

21   SHAPIRO, KARL. "The Retreat of W.H. Auden," in his In De-
      fense of Ignorance. New York: Random House, pp. 115–41.
           Tries to define what is "Audenesque," calls Auden "the
      master of the Middle Style," and thinks our age will be
      "the age of Auden." Shapiro compares Auden to various
      poets (particularly Eliot, whom Shapiro dislikes) and
      illustrates liberally from Auden's Collected Poetry (1945).

22   STRAVINSKY, IGOR AND ROBERT CRAFT. "The Rake's Progress," in
      Memories and Commentaries. London: Faber and Faber, pp.
      154–76; Garden City: Doubleday, pp. 144–67.

An account by Stravinsky of working with Auden on The Rake's Progress; includes letters from Auden to Stravinsky and comments by Stravinsky on Auden's personality.

23 SYMONS, JULIAN. The Thirties: A Dream Revolved. London: The Cresset Press, passim.
   A general background review of the thirties in which Auden is a prominent figure. Sees him as both expressive of the age and an expression of the age and tries to communicate some of the feelings about the poems and plays as they appeared on the scene in contrast to their collection in books.

24 THOMPSON, E.P. "Outside the Whale," in Out of Apathy. London: Stevens, pp. 141-94.
   Accuses Auden of default, of giving up instead of confronting, of recoiling "from a social reality...found inexplicable or unbearable." Evidence of this regression appears in Auden's revisions of Spain and September 1, 1939. See especially pp. 147-56.

1961 A BOOKS - NONE

1961 B SHORTER WRITINGS

1 BLACKBURN, THOMAS. "W.H. Auden," in The Price of an Eye. London: Longmans, pp. 85-98.
   "The artist only deserves his name if he wrestles from the unconscious certain truths which have relevance to a man and his life." Auden fails to do that; thus Blackburn lists numerous instances of his failure.

2 BLUESTONE, MAX. "The Iconographic Sources of Auden's 'Musee des Beaux Arts.'" Modern Language Notes, 76 (April), 331-36.
   A reply in part to Charney's article (1960.B3) asserting that Auden's view is one of "ironic humor." Bluestone accepts irony but not humor as part of the tone. Chiefly the article traces all the images in "Musee des Beaux Arts" to Breughel's paintings and also a good many other images in Auden that gain meaning from their relevance to Breughel.

3 CAVANAUGH, WILLIAM C. "Coriolanus and The Ascent of F-6: Similarities in Theme and Supporting Detail." Drama Critique, 4 (February), 9-17.

   Draws parallels between Coriolanus and The Ascent of F6
in respect to the mother-son theme and the power theme by
comparing characters, actions, and structure in the two
plays.

4   COX, R.G. "The Poetry of W.H. Auden," in The Modern Age:
    The Pelican Guide to English Literature, vol. 7. Edited
    by Boris Ford. Harmondsworth: Penguin, pp. 373-93.
       The variety of opinions about Auden (that he is a
    satirist, a romantic, a poet of general ideas, a writer
    of light verse) rises out of the various stages his own
    "thought and feeling have passed through in thirty
    years...." Summarizes with running commentary Auden's
    poetic and dramatic works, considers his "successful"
    poems and his "incidental and fragmentary brilliances,"
    and concludes that "he has never gathered up and concen-
    trated all his powers in a major achievement...." Re-
    printed: 1963.B7.

5   FORD, HUGH D. "British Poetry of the Spanish Civil War."
    Ph.D. dissertation, University of Pennsylvania, pp. 336-
    47.
       Studies the response of various poets, including Auden,
    to the Spanish Civil War, which had a cathartic effect
    leading "to repudiation of the political life." The poetry
    produced, if not "technically distinguished," was "at
    least morally earnest." See pp. 336-47. Abstracted in
    Dissertation Abstracts, 23 (September 1962), 1017-18.

6   HOGGART, RICHARD. "Introduction," in W.H. Auden: A
    Selection. London: Hutchinson Educational, pp. 13-41.
       Written for use in British schools. Places Auden in
    his family and school background relating it to his poems,
    then takes up the period of the thirties and Auden's con-
    cern for "objectivity," and finally discusses Auden's
    forms and ideas with a few close readings. Partially re-
    printed (all but first four pages): 1964.A4.

7   HOOPER, A.G., AND C.J.D. HARVEY. "Commentary," in Talking
    of Poetry. Cape Town: Oxford University Press, pp. 183-
    86.
       A line by line close reading of "Their Lonely Betters."
    Since man is partly irrational and instinctive and there-
    fore irresolute, he knows that the non-human world is
    better off without the responsibilities created by lan-
    guage.

8   ISHERWOOD, CHRISTOPHER. "A Conversation on Tape." London
     Magazine, n.s., 1 (June), 41-58.
         Interview recorded at Isherwood's home in California
     contains brief comments about collaboration with Auden on
     plays, about Auden as a learned man, and about Auden
     generally as a person.

9   JANET, SISTER M., S.C.L. "W.H. Auden: Two Poems in Sequence."
     Renascence, 13 (Spring), 115-18.
         "The Sea and the Mirror" and "For the Time Being" not
     only share themes and central concerns but the second is a
     sequel to the first. Auden first brings "the artist to the
     edge of the abyss" in "The Sea and the Mirror," and then
     in "For the Time Being" shows ways other than art for
     completing the journey.

10   MANDER, JOHN. "Must We Burn Auden?" in The Writer and Com-
     mitment. London: Secker & Warburg, pp. 24-70.
         A survey of negative views on Auden, even those not
     meant to be negative, concentrating on three critiques by
     Alvarez, Beach, and Orwell. Mander's defense rests on
     acknowledging the aptness of these critiques but arguing
     the thesis that Auden is "best when he is most himself,
     when he has succeeded in constructing...a world of his own."
     Then examines Auden's work in Poems, Look, Stranger! and
     Spain for strengths and weaknesses from this point of view.

11   SANDEEN, ERNEST. "Facing the Muse." Poetry, 97 (March),
     380-86.
         Homage to Clio will not change the view of either those
     who like Auden or those who dislike him. It has many of
     the characteristics we expect. Auden does, however, have
     new "awareness of his Muse." Although he has always writ-
     ten under the Muse of History, he now makes Clio the sub-
     ject as well as the point of view. This change is a
     "shift in the angle of his perception."

12   SCOTT, NATHAN A. "The Poetry of Auden." London Magazine,
     8 (January), 44-63.
         Reprint of 1959.B6.

13   SPEARS, MONROE K. "Auden in the Fifties: Rites of Homage."
     Sewanee Review, 69 (Summer), 375-98.
         Auden's view of the creative act as a "rite of homage"
     seems different from his earlier views of it as a game,
     as psychotherapy, or as a mirror. Spears believes it
     merely a change in emphasis or tone. He sees numerous
     pieces of bad verse in Homage to Clio, looking at it from

the perspective of Auden's previous works; but the book
marks the end of a decade that "forms a unity." He also
again reviews Auden's work as that of a satirist.

1962 A   BOOKS

1   BLAIR, JOHN G. "W.H. Auden: His Characteristic Poetic Mode."
Ph.D. dissertation, Brown University.
Auden's mode is "anti-romantic," resulting in a verse
that is generally didactic, impersonal, and "unserious."
Opera especially interests Auden as a genre that "discour-
ages the audience from taking the world of the work of
art with romantic overseriousness." Abstracted in Dissertation Abstracts, 24 (December 1963), 2473-74.

2   ROSEN, AARON H. "The Critical Prose of W.H. Auden." Ph.D.
dissertation, University of California, Berkeley.
Studies Auden's intellectual development as ascertained
by his critical prose, 1926-1957, a development marked by
his aesthetic and "extra-aesthetic" interests. Abstracted
in Dissertation Abstracts, 24 (May 1964), 4703.

1962 B   SHORTER WRITINGS

1   AHERN, ECKOE M. "There May Be Many Answers." English Journal, 51 (December), 657-58.
Outlines a lesson plan for teaching high school sopho-
mores the "individual interpretation" of poetry, using
Auden's "O What Is That Sound?" as an example.

2   BERRY, FRANCIS. "Some Recent Voices," in Poetry and the
Physical Voice. London: Routledge, pp. 185-88.
Discusses the value of listening to the physical voice
of the poet speaking his own poems and particularly the
changes in Auden's voice as a reflection of changes in
his printed style over the years.

3   BLOOMFIELD, B.C. "W.H. Auden's First Book." Library, 5th
series, 17 (June), 152-54.
Describes in detail Auden's first book of poems printed
by Stephen Spender in 1928-29 and variations in ten sur-
viving copies. The book was given a professional look by
the Holywell Press Oxford who finished and bound the book
for Spender.

4   BULLOUGH, GEOFFREY. Mirror of Minds. Toronto: University
of Toronto Press, pp. 234-42.

Discusses the influence of psychology on Auden's verse,
particularly that of Freud and Adler as related to the
concepts of love and the self. Auden believes the poet
must point out the errors of the individual and of society
and show them how to improve.

5   COOK, F.W. "Primordial Auden," Essays in Criticism, 12
(October), 402-12.
    Analyzes Paid on Both Sides to clarify some of its
"obscurities." Shows the relationship of the parts to the
whole and sees the final chorus as the summing up of themes
in the play. "Primordial" has to do with Auden's view of
contemporary society with the layers "peeled away."

6   DAVIDSON, MICHAEL. The World, the Flesh and Myself. London:
Arthur Barker, pp. 126-30.
    An account of Davidson's acquaintance with Auden be-
ginning when the poet was sixteen. Auden at that age
seemed much older and impressively intelligent, already
didactic; to Davidson his smallest remarks were "inspired
wisdom." Recounts also a few anecdotes of Auden's later
years.

7   DEMETILLO, RICAREDO. "The High Game of Poetry in W.H. Auden,"
in The Authentic Voice of Poetry. Diliman: University of
the Philippines, pp. 195-211.
    Discusses Auden's technique as "the high game of
poetry." Auden's language "is always idiomatic..., only
refined and made wonderfully pliable." Sees Auden as
apparently frivolous but really "a moral genius."

8   GERSTENBERGER, DONNA. "Poetry and Politics: The Verse Drama
of Auden and Isherwood." Modern Drama, 5 (September),
123-32.
    The values of Auden's experiments with verse play lie
in their "defining limits and in exploring possibilities."
Ascent of F6 is the most unified of the plays; but it, too,
like the others, fails as drama. Argues, however, for
their place "in the development of modern verse drama,
...an attempt to convey wholly modern content in the most
immediately relevant terms."

9   HAEFFNER, PAUL. "Auden and Ella Wheeler Wilcox." Notes &
Queries, n.s. 9 (March), 110-11.
    Auden's poem "O What Is That Sound" has a parallel in
Wilcox's "The Arrival." Comments on other parallels be-
tween Auden's style and other "woman poets."

1962

10   HAGOPIAN, JOHN V. "Exploring Auden's Limestone Landscape."
        Die Neueren Sprachen, n.s. 11 (June), 255-60.
           Reviews the comments and explications of "In Praise of
        Limestone," points out their inadequacies, and offers a
        new explication. The poem celebrates "existential
        humanism" and is anti-Christian; it is an address which
        demonstrates the values of "the limestone landscape."
        Critics are baffled by this poem because it professes
        beliefs Auden himself no longer holds.

11   KHAN, B.A. The English Poetic Drama. Aligarh: Muslim
        University, pp. 47-51.
           Accounts for Auden's plays as an experiment for at-
        tracting larger audiences. Treats each play in turn,
        commenting on its dramatic qualities, its stylistic ele-
        ments, and its use as propaganda. Auden used plays as a
        means rather than as an end, and his giving up play writ-
        ing "meant that he did not go to drama with any delibera-
        tion."

12   McDOWELL, FREDERICK P. "'The Situation of Our Time': Auden
        in His American Phase," in Aspects of American Poetry.
        Edited by Richard M. Ludwig. Columbus: Ohio State
        University Press, pp. 223-55.
           On This Island and the poems after it mark a technique
        based on the "rhythms of speech" and are therefore able
        to carry Auden's "increasingly intricate thought." Lists
        Auden's "indispensable" titles; studies in detail "New
        Year Letter" and "The Sea and the Mirror"; and discusses
        briefly "For the Time Being" and "The Age of Anxiety."
        Excerpts reprinted: 1964.A4.

13   _____. "Subtle, Various Ornamental, Clever: Auden in
        His Recent Poetry." Wisconsin Studies in Contemporary
        Literature, 3 (Fall), 29-44.
           Auden's poetry of the fifties bears comparison with his
        own earlier poetry, contrary to the opinions of some
        critics. Auden has become confident in his beliefs; thus
        his Christianity forms the background of his work, rather
        than the subject of it. Nevertheless, his speech is more
        tentative from "a rooted distrust of 'all sane affirmative
        speech....'" Discusses groups of poems from Auden's latest
        volumes, offering brief descriptions of their themes and
        subjects.

14   REPLOGLE, JUSTIN. "The Gang Myth in Auden's Early Poetry."
        Journal of English and Germanic Philology, 61 No. 3, 481-
        95.

Auden's early poetry employs a "private myth," and therefore elucidation of this myth also elucidates much of the obscurity in these poems. Traces the evolution of the myth from Auden's childhood through his friendship with Isherwood and describes its basic features.

15   SPEARS, MONROE K. "W.H. Auden at Swarthmore." Swarthmore College Bulletin, 59 (March), 1-6.
      Describes Auden's activities at Swarthmore and his role there as "a regular teacher in the normal academic estab-lishment." Discusses a number of Auden's articles and talks addressed to students and also public lectures. As teacher Auden showed "a flair for the unexpected approach." His examination on Elizabethan Literature asked, "Explain why the devil is (a) sad and (b) honest." Auden reviewed a few plays produced by students, suggesting that college theaters "spend time on noncommercial plays like Jonson's Alchemist or Cocteau's Orphee." Spears thinks Auden's residence at Swarthmore "more productive than any equiv-alent period of his whole career, before or since."

16   WALLACE-CRABBE, CHRIS. "Auden's New Year Letter and the Fate of Long Poems." Melbourne Critical Review, 5: 128-36.
      Despite the consensus of critics and poets themselves that long poems are now practically impossible, Auden has made continual efforts at "poetic structures more exten-sive than the lyric and the short meditation." Auden's "Letter to Lord Byron" is a kind of preparation for New Year Letter, for in it he learned to achieve a consistency of voice and form and also "by-passed" Eliot and Pound, "going over their heads to a poetic mode established in the past." Although New Year Letter fails, Auden created a "manner capable of magnanimity."

17   WHEELWRIGHT, PHILIP. "Two Ways of Metaphor," in his Metaphor and Reality. Bloomington: Indiana University Press, pp. 86-87.
      Uses Auden's "The Fall of Rome" to illustrate a combi-nation of epiphor and diaphor (two different semantic movements of metaphor).

1963 A BOOKS

*1   LOOSE, JOHN H. "W.H. Auden's Poetic: A Study of the Rela-tionship Between His Aesthetic Theory and His Theological Point of View." Ph.D. dissertation, University of Chicago (Divinity School).
      Not seen. Cited in 1972.A2.

1963

2   SPEARS, MONROE K. The Poetry of W.H. Auden: The Disenchanted
     Island. New York: Oxford University Press, 394 pp.
        Contains index of Auden's published poems by title and
     first line. First line index gives history of the printing
     of the poem, including, therefore, title changes. A kind
     of reader's guide with a mixture of biography and analyses
     of poems on most of Auden's works to 1962. Concludes with
     chapter on opera and criticism. Reprinted: 1968.A4; ex-
     cerpts: 1968.B12; "The Sea and the Mirror": 1964.A4.

1963 B SHORTER WRITINGS

1   BROOKE-ROSE, CHRISTINE. "Notes on the Metre of Auden's 'The
     Age of Anxiety.'" Essays in Criticism, 13 (July), 253-64.
        Detailed comparison of Auden's metrics in "The Age of
     Anxiety" with Anglo-Saxon alliterative measures.

2   CALLAN, EDWARD. "Auden's New Year Letter: A New Style of
     Architecture." Renascence, 16 (Fall), 13-19.
        Treats "New Year Letter" as Auden's first experimenting
     with new structure and styles for long poems. Discusses
     each section of the poem from the thesis that it repre-
     sents the viewpoint of Kierkegaard's Aesthetic, Ethical,
     or Religious person. Reprinted: 1964.A4.

3   _____. "Auden on Christianity and Criticism." The
     Christian Scholar, 46 (Summer), 168-73.
        Reviews Auden's literary theory as expressed in The
     Dyer's Hand. The distinctive character of Auden's
     criticism derives from his "familiarity with modern
     speculative thought" and "fascination with, and profound
     knowledge of, the techniques of his craft."

4   CHITTICK, V.L.O. "Angry Young Poet of the Thirties."
     Dalhousie Review, 43 (Spring), 85-97.
        Unlike latter day "angries" Auden knew what angered him
     and the cure for it. Chittick demonstrates in example
     after example the course of Auden's anger and the
     remedies he proposed until the late thirties when the
     wrath in Auden becomes "righteous indignation." Belief
     in humanistic love as the redemptive power for man's
     social ills changes to belief in Christian love.

5   COOK, FREDERICK W. "The Allotropy of the Auden Group." Ph.D.
     dissertation, University of Nottingham.
        Not seen. Cited in 1972.A2.

6   COX, C.B., AND A.E. DYSON. "W.H. Auden: Spain 1937," in
    Modern Poetry. London: Edward Arnold, pp. 90-97.
        Auden's poem "Spain" is famous for having given "strik-
    ing artistic form to the instinctive apprehensions of a
    whole generation...." Has background information on the
    international political climate, on Auden's cultural
    origins, and on his personal traits. Describes and judges
    the poem's weaknesses and strengths.

7   COX, R.G. "The Poetry of W.H. Auden," in The Modern Age:
    The Pelican Guide to English Literature, vol. 7. Second
    edition. Edited by Boris Ford. Harmondsworth: Penguin,
    pp. 377-93.
        Reprint of 1961.B4.

8   DASGUPTA, N. "Auden," in Modern English Poetry. Delhi:
    Kitab Mihal, pp. 58-73.
        Analyzes with regret the differences between Auden's
    work of the thirties and his work of the forties, for he
    has replaced "simple and lucid poems" with difficult
    ones, "packing them with supplementary notes in prose and
    verse." He has lost his lyricism and "deep insight into
    human characters," and has changed his position from one
    with common men to "stabilisation of the existing social
    structure." Dasgupta finds the seeds of this change in
    the early poems and traces their sprouting and growth to
    Auden's "Faith, that Natural Law exists and that we can
    have knowledge of it; Doubt, that our knowledge can ever
    be perfect or unmixed with error."

9   DRIVER, TOM F. "Auden's View of History in 'For the Time
    Being.'" Journal of Bible and Religion, 31 (January),
    3-8.
        Auden employs the biblical view of history, which sees
    the past event re-occurring in the present. This view,
    along with "love for the tangible practicalities of finite
    historical existence" is Protestant rather than Catholic.

10 EMPSON, WILLIAM. "Early Auden." Review (Oxford), 5
    (February), 32-34.
        Admires Auden's skill in the thirties: "there is
    always this curious curl of the tongue in his voice." He
    could write about socialism "without sounding phoney," as
    if he were laughing "at you for not being more sensible."

11 KINNEY, ARTHUR F. "Auden, Bruegel, and 'Musee des Beaux
    Arts.'" College English, 24 (April), 529-31.

Inspects paintings hanging in a special Bruegel alcove in the Musees Royaux des Beaux-Arts, Brussels, for evidence of a source for Auden's imagery in the poem. Relates some particular images in the poems to four paintings.

12   OHMANN, RICHARD M. "Auden's Sacred Awe." Commonweal, 78 (31 May), 279-81.
Reviews briefly Auden's career and literary reputation and then The Dyer's Hand as "fifteen years' worth of major comments on literature." In it is the reason Auden's work has not mummified: "A sense of the power and meaning that permeates experience, ...animates the abstractions, and... should preserve him, finally, from the charge of ideological fickleness." Reprinted: 1964.A4.

13   POGGIOLI, RENATO. "Decadence in Miniature." Massachusetts Review, 4 (Spring), 531-62.
In "The Epigoni" Auden pokes fun at decadent poets, both "those who stand for Rome's bygone doomsday and those who stand for the forthcoming 'last judgment' of the West." Only pp. 537-41 apply to Auden.

14   REPLOGLE, JUSTIN. "Auden's Homage to Thalia." Bucknell Review, 11 (March), 98-117.
Relates Auden's "comic sense" to his concerns about art and human nature. Compares the early comedy with the later and offers examples from Auden's later works which mingle the serious and the comic.

15   STRAVINSKY, IGOR AND ROBERT CRAFT. Dialogues and a Diary. Garden City: Doubleday, passim.
Dedicated to "Wystan Auden," the book relates anecdotes of Auden in Italy and the United States in the fifties and early sixties, revealing his interests and idiosyncracies.

16   WRIGHT, BASIL. "Britten and Documentary." Musical Times, 104 (November), 779-80.
Personal reminiscence of Britten and Auden working together on films (GPO Film Unit, later Crown Film Unit) beginning in 1935. "O, lurcher-loving collier" ("Madrigal") was apparently Auden's first piece that Britten set to music.

1964 A BOOKS

1   BLOOMFIELD, B.C. W.H. Auden: A Bibliography: the early
    years through 1955. Charlottesville: University Press
    of Virginia, 171 pp.
        Foreward by W.H. Auden. An early version of 1972.A2.

2   EVERETT, BARBARA. Auden. Writers and Critics. Edinburgh:
    Oliver & Boyd, 117 pp.
        Stresses the unity of Auden's work, treating it chrono-
    logically to reveal its development and employing Auden's
    prose writings to elucidate the poems. Auden's work has
    "continuity; like the 'questing hero' himself, its motive
    principle remains very little changed, though it moves
    through rapidly-changing landscapes of thought and feel-
    ing." Auden tries "to verify the personal and the fabu-
    lous in terms of the 'real.'"

3   GREENBERG, HERBERT S. "Quest for the Necessary: A Study of
    the Poetry of W.H. Auden." Ph.D. dissertation, University
    of Wisconsin.
        Shows the unity of Auden's work by examining his atti-
    tudes toward love as an explanation of "his shifts of
    commitment." An early version of 1968.A3.

4   SPEARS, MONROE K., ed. Auden: A Collection of Critical
    Essays. Twentieth Century Views. Englewood Cliffs, New
    Jersey: Prentice-Hall, 184 pp.
        Most of the essays collected are from the fifties and
    early sixties; five are from 1950's, six from 1960's and
    two from the thirties. All are favorable to Auden.
    Spears' introduction gives a brief history of criticism
    of Auden both favorable and unfavorable, as is standard
    in the Prentice-Hall series, and describes succinctly the
    essays in the collection.

1964 B SHORTER WRITINGS

1   BROOKS, CLEANTH. "A Descriptive Chart of the Disenchanted
    Island." Sewanee Review, 72 (April-June), 300-306.
        Reviews Spears' The Poetry of W.H. Auden (1963.A2) as
    "not only serviceable but acute and discerning." De-
    scribes the book, praises Spears' honesty and intelli-
    gence, and stresses those aspects of Auden which need
    such a commentary.

2   _____. "W.H. Auden as a Critic." Kenyon Review, 26
    (Winter), 173-89.

1964

Auden is "the poet of civilization" and reveals that
fact in his reviews and criticism, most of which has to do
with man in his "economic or sociological or psychological
context." Describes and discusses the contents and worth
of Auden's various essays throughout his career. Concludes that Auden is one of the "soundest" of critics as
well as exciting. Reprinted.: 1971.B2; 1972.B4.

3 FIEDLER, LESLIE A. "A Kind of Solution: The Situation of
    Poetry Now." Kenyon Review, 26 (Winter), 54-79.
        Describes, classifies, compares the best known poets
    of the early sixties. Discusses Auden on pp. 61-63.
    Auden's move to America was a "second birth."

4 FRASER, GEORGE S. "Auden: The Composite Giant." Shenandoah,
    15 (Summer), 46-59.
        Takes Graves' term about Auden as a "synthetic" or
    composite poet and transforms it into a term of praise.
    This characteristic of "compositeness" leads to a com-
    parison with Dryden, especially with his shifts of loyal-
    ties. Discusses also Auden's "composite voice": He is a
    "great English poet who is a great American poet..., two
    voices, two rhythms are fused."

5 FULLER, JOHN. "Early Auden: An Allegory of Love." Review
    (Oxford), pp. 11-12, 83-90.
        A review of The Poetry of W.H. Auden by Monroe K. Spears
    1963.A2. Although Spears supplies much information that is
    "indispensable," he omits "the interpretive spark." The
    material belongs as annotations in "some hypothetical
    Complete Auden." Praises the book's scholarship but calls
    for "a persuasively defensive work" on the best poems.

6 GALINSKY, HANS. "The Expatriate Poet's Style: With Reference
    to T.S. Eliot and W.H. Auden," in English Studies Today.
    Third Series, Pp. 215-26.
        Auden's use of his "expatriation" as a stylistic re-
    source extends and intensifies what Eliot touched on in
    Sweeney Agonistes; both try for comical or satirical ef-
    fects, Eliot by retention and Auden by adoption of Ameri-
    canisms. Reprinted, according to Bloomfield (1972.A2),
    with altered title in Galinsky's Amerika und Europa.
    Berlin: Langenscheit, 1968, pp. 102-10.

7 GROSS, HARVEY. "The Generation of Auden," in his Sound and
    Form in Modern Poetry. Ann Arbor: University of Michigan
    Press, pp. 247-301.

Treats Auden exclusively on pp. 249-61. Studies
Auden's prosody over the whole range of his verse from
1936 to 1960.

8   HARDY, BARBARA. "The Reticence of W.H. Auden." Review
(Oxford), Nos. 11-12, 54-64.
Describes the different forms of Auden's reticence from
"strident imperatives" to "exaggerated carelessness."
Argues that Auden's use of these devices does not mean he
lacks feeling or undervalues personal experiences.

9   HAZARD, FORREST E. "The Auden Group and the Group Theatre:
The Dramatic Theories of Rupert Doone, W.H. Auden, Chris-
topher Isherwood, Louis MacNeice, Stephen Spender, and
Cecil Day Lewis." Ph.D. dissertation, The University of
Wisconsin.
Relates the principles governing productions by the
Group Theatre to other experiments in drama and evaluates
the Doone-Auden achievement. Abstracted in Dissertation
Abstracts, 25 (September 1964), 1913-14.

10 IZZO, CARLO. "The Poetry of W.H. Auden," translated by
Camilla Roatta, in Auden: A Collection of Critical Essays. Edited by Monroe K. Spears. Englewwod Cliffs, New
Jersey: Prentice Hall, pp. 125-41. Translated and
abridged from Izzo's introduction to Poesie di W.H. Auden
(Parma: Guande, 1952) and from his Storia della Literature Inglese, vol. 2 (Milan: Nuova Accademia, 1963).
Personal reminiscences of Auden in Italy and a general
commentary on his place in English and American literature, his personal and literary characteristics, and his
themes.

11 KALLMAN, CHESTER. "Looking and Thinking Back," in The Rake's
Progress (Recording). New York: Columbia M3S 710/M3L
310, pp. 33-34.
Booklet accompanying the recording; includes Vera
Stravinsky's account of the opening night, "La Prima
Assoluta," p. 8. Reprinted: more readily available in
1966.B17; 1967.B14.

12 MAGNUSSON, SIGURDUR A. "Auden in Iceland." Iceland Review,
2, no. 3, 30.
About Auden's and MacNeice's visit to Iceland in 1936.
Quotes a lengthy passage from Auden's letter to his wife
about how he came to write Letters from Iceland in verse.
It is "a candid and unsentimental account" rather resented
by the Icelanders; Magnusson defends the account as

1964

accurate. The article reprints "Journey to Iceland" and a
poem written on the occasion of his second visit in April
1963 or 1964, "Iceland Revisited," dedicated to the British
Ambassador to Iceland, Basil Boothby and his wife Susan.

13   MARKEN, RONALD. "Power and Conflict in 'The Ascent of F.6.'"
     Discourse, 7 (Summer), 277-82.
        The dominant symbol in The Ascent of F6, the mountain,
     has a quality shared by every mountain, ugly or beautiful,
     "an unmistakable aura of lofty power." Since the corollary
     of any kind of power is conflict, the mountain as power
     clarifies action on all levels in the play.

*14 MORGAN, KATHLEEN E. "Christian Themes in English Poetry of
     the Twentieth Century." Ph.D. dissertation, University
     of Liverpool.
        Not seen. Cited in 1972.A2.

15   OSTROFF, ANTHONY, ed. "On W.H. Auden's 'A Change of Air,'"
     in his The Contemporary Poet as Artist and Critic. Boston:
     Little, Brown, pp. 167-87.
        Reprint of 1964.B16.

16   _____. "A Symposium on W.H. Auden's 'A Change of Air.'"
     Kenyon Review, 26 (Winter), 190-208.
        Interpretive commentary on Auden's "A Change of Air" by
     George P. Elliott, Karl Shapiro, and Stephen Spender fol-
     lowed by Auden's comments on their responses to his poem.
     Reprinted: 1964.B15.

17   POVEY, JOHN F. "The Oxford Group: A Study of the Poetry of
     W.H. Auden, Stephen Spender, C. Day Lewis and Louis
     MacNeice." Ph.D. dissertation, Michigan State University.
        Assesses the work of the "Group," accounting for the
     lessening critical acclaim by a gradual "deterioration"
     of skills. Abstracted in Dissertation Abstracts, 25 (May
     1965), 6633-34.

18   REED, JOHN R. Old School Ties. Syracuse: Syracuse Univer-
     sity Press, pp. 107-109, 206-207.
        Examines in a general way the influence of public school
     education on Auden and his work, one writer among thirty-
     four others. Most of the attitudes discussed are anta-
     gonistic toward the system. Auden casts society in the
     "aspect of a public school, and the old boy is trying to
     establish a new order within the old system."

1965

19 REPLOGLE, JUSTIN. "The Auden Group." Wisconsin Studies in
    Contemporary Literature, 5 (Summer), 133-50.
        The birth, growth, and demise of Auden's group, placing
    his Marxism in perspective and defining the ideas on art
    and politics held in common.

20 WARNER, ALAN. "W.H. Auden's 'Autumn Song.'" Critical Sur-
    vey, 1 (Summer), 203-205.
        Warner contrasts his own analysis of "Autumn Song:
    with views expressed in a discussion at the Critical
    Quarterly Conference in Bristol (April 1964). He comments
    on tone, imagery, influences, and theme to make fully
    conscious his intuitive grasp of the poem.

21 WEATHERHEAD, A. KINGSLEY. "The Good Place in the latest
    Poems of W.H. Auden." Twentieth Century Literature, 10
    (October), 99-107.
        Uses Auden's last poems to illustrate his "creation of
    an Eden out of the materials of ordinary...living."
    Auden's success is in his ability to "poetize" the usual
    or the everyday.

22 WEST, WILLIAM C. "Concepts of Reality in the Poetic Drama
    of W.B. Yeats, W.H. Auden, and T.S. Eliot." Ph.D. dis-
    sertation, Stanford University.
        Compares the beliefs of Auden, Yeats, and Eliot as the
    basis for their "concepts of reality," representing the
    "major positions between the subjective and objective
    poles of art." Abstracted in Dissertation Abstracts, 25
    (April 1965), 6120-21.

1965 A BOOKS

1 BLAIR, JOHN G. The Poetic Art of W.H. Auden. Princeton:
   University Press, 210 pp.
        Convinced that previous criticism has emphasized ideas
   in Auden's poetry at the expense of the art, Blair states
   his aims: "My interest is in building out of an informed
   familiarity with Auden's work a sense of the fundamental
   aesthetic attitudes and practices that have guided his
   poetry to date." Sees the body of Auden's poetry as
   fundamentally whole and consistent; sees Auden as an anti-
   Romantic and a moralist. Explores first the "anti-
   Romantic impulses"; then the habits of Auden's imagination
   (use of allegory, dramatic convention, and poetic forms
   an techniques); and Auden's contribution to opera, in
   which Blair finds "a final epitomizing figure for his
   poetic mode."

1965

2   DEWSNAP, TERENCE. The Major Poems of W.H. Auden. Monarch
    Notes and Study Guides, 791-94. New York: Monarch
    Press, 90 pp.
        Has background and biographical information and notes
    on Auden's work. Includes a set of sample essay questions
    and answers for college students and a brief bibliography.
    Printed also as The Poetry of W.H. Auden and is exactly
    the same book.

3   JOHNSON, RICHARD A. "A Reading of W.H. Auden's Poetry."
    Ph.D. dissertation, Cornell University.
        Analyzes style in numerous poems and finds Auden con-
    sistently anti-Romantic. Abstracted in Dissertation Ab-
    stracts, 28 (August 1967), 680-A.

1965 B   SHORTER WRITINGS

1   BAIN, CARL E. "W.H. Auden." Emory University Quarterly, 21
    (Spring), 45-58.
        The most prominent element in Auden's moral landscape
    is the "earthly City." It figures as a life existing be-
    tween the natural and the historical, a dual but insig-
    nificant and "essentially humdrum everyday life." The
    role of the poet in such a city is private, not social;
    the poem is directed at the reader by the poet. When
    these three meet, the "poetic experience" occurs whatever
    the social conditions.

2   BLAIR, JOHN G. "W.H. Auden: The Poem as Performance."
    Shenandoah, 16 (Spring), 55-66.
        Responds to the criticism of Joseph Warren Beach and
    other similar critics by contrasting their aesthetic
    theories with Auden's. They see poems as verbal structures
    with only one possible basic meaning; Auden "treats the
    poem as a performance," testing it "from the audience's
    point of view."

3   CALLAN, EDWARD. "Allegory in Auden's The Age of Anxiety."
    Twentieth Century Literature, 10 (January), 155-65.
        Auden attempts to present man's basic problem, his
    "anxiety in time," as "a dramatic allegory." Works out in
    detail the psychological and spiritual levels of The Age
    of Anxiety.

4   _____. "Auden and Kierkegaard. The Artistic Framework
    of For the Time Being." The Christian Scholar, 48 (Fall),
    211-23.

Auden both utilizes and departs from the traditional
nativity play. He uses the traditional scriptures and
"adds insights from modern psychologists, philosophers,
and theologians." The inspiration and influence of Kierkegaard extend even into the structure, for Auden drama-
tizes such concepts as "Kierkegaard's concept of anxiety
as the threshold of faith." A close-reading essay of
For the Time Being.

5   ELLIOTT, ALISTAIR. "Auden Is Good." Essays in Criticism, 15
    (October), 462-70.
        Reviews Barbara Everett's Auden, 1964.A2, surveys the
    recent critical attitudes, and contends that we are still
    awaiting the right critic for Auden.

6   FORD, HUGH D. "Auden's 'Spain': End of an Era," in his A
    Poets' War: British Poets and the Spanish Civil War.
    Philadelphia: University of Pennsylvania Press, pp. 206-
    15, 288.
        "Spain" was Auden's only and final statement on the
    Spanish Civil War and also his last "conspicuously"
    Marxist poem. Discusses numerous details and passages in
    the poem and a few of the revisions Auden made for subse-
    quent printings.

7   FOWLER, HELEN. "The Faces and Places of Auden." Approach,
    57 (Fall), 6-14.
        An essay on how-to-read Auden's poetry. Elaborates the
    theme of Auden's proclamation about the wisdom and nice-
    ness of "private faces in public places." The problems
    for Auden and for his readers have been "problems of in-
    timacy." Auden has always known his audience from the
    beginning and attempted an intimate relationship with it.
    The reader "forms a twosome with his I"; and Auden employs
    "the undefined pronoun" to establish intimacy. His was a
    public face in a public place during the thirties, "warn-
    ing against approaching catastrophes." Afterwards, dis-
    illusioned about the role of bard, he grew "more resolutely"
    private.

8   FRASER, GEORGE S. The Modern Writer and His World. New
    York: Criterion Books, passim.
        References to Auden are scattered throughout, but he
    receives concentrated attention on pp. 297-304. It sets
    him in his time, considers the rhetorical influence of
    Hopkins on the poets of the thirties, and assesses
    Auden's rank as a poet (who else is there?). "Nobody is
    quite sure that he is a major poet; and nobody is quite
    sure, if not, why not."

1965

9 GHOSH, PRABODH CHANDRA. "The Ascent of F6 and Fry," in Poetry and Religion as Drama. Calcutta: World Press Private, pp. 185-96.

Auden and Fry make use of Murder in the Cathedral, Brecht's epic theater, German expressionism, film technique, and the music hall in The Ascent of F6. The play's "frantic search for form" is important as an experiment in modern drama even if not altogether successful. Ghosh enumerates various levels of meaning and outlines the structure of the play, which reaches "a truly tragic combination of pity and irony." The remainder of the essay discusses Fry and some of his other plays.

10 GRUBB, FREDERICK. "English Auden and the 30's Ethos," in A Vision of Reality. London: Chatto & Windus, pp. 137-57; passim.

Critics have been unfair to Auden because they do not "distinguish between the intention of the poets and their meaning for us today." But Auden's "liberal vision" is still valid; for he criticises authority and "Idealism" and "makes us conscious, sensitive, and responsible."

11 _____. "Scowling at a Cigarette: The 30's Poets." Poetry Review (London), 56, 36-43.

A review of Robin Skelton's The Poets of the Thirties (Penguin Books), it comments briefly on Auden's poems selected for the book; but mostly the comments are directed at the choices of poems by all the poets in the anthology. Grubb would have chosen other poems and arranged them differently; anyway Eliot had already taken care of most of the "themes" arranged by Skelton. This review has some background information (not biographical) on the poets.

12 GUSTAFSON, RICHARD. "The Paragon Style: Frost and Auden." Poet and Critic, 2 (Fall), 35-42.

Both Auden and Frost exemplify the "paragon style" by their refinement of colloquial, or "ordinary," language. "Their language is the language of the tribe.... They are our modern classicists."

13 HARDY, BARBARA. "Spears on Auden." Essays in Criticism, 15 (April), 230-38.

Review of W.H. Auden: The Disenchanted Island (1963.A2). Spears' book is useful for background study or glosses on erudite passages but sacrifices foreground. Disagrees with various analyses of poems because the emphasis is on form and ideas rather than feeling.

14   HARRIS, HENRY.   "The Symbols and Imagery of Hawk and Kestrel
      in the Poetry of Auden and Day Lewis in the "Thirties.'"
      Zietschrift fur Anglistik und Amerikanistik, 13 (July),
      276-85.
          Auden and Day Lewis employ images of "Hawk" and "Kes-
      trel" usually in two ways: "(1) close, realistic observa-
      tion of the natural world contrasted with urban...elements
      and didactic Marxist comment..., or (2)...symbolic phe-
      nomena in imaginary, fantasy environments...with a strong
      mythical or...allegoric content." Harris compares the
      different attitudes of the two poets as evidenced in par-
      ticular poems. He finds the projection of a "detached ob-
      server of the human condition and the physical world"
      related to the poets' own position, their "separation
      from the bourgeois social structure."

15   HOGGART, RICHARD, "W.H. Auden," in British Writers and Their
      Work, No. 5. Edited by J.W. Robinson. Lincoln, Nebraska:
      University of Nebraska Press, pp. 71-118.
          An updating of 1957.A2 to include Auden's latest poems
      in the chapter "In the Meantime." Also a revised bibli-
      ography by J.W. Robinson. Text reprinted: 1970.B11.

16   HOSKINS, KATHERINE B. "Today the Struggle: A Study of
      Literature and Politics in England During the Spanish
      Civil War." Ph.D. dissertation, Columbia University.
          A general discussion of writers with a political pur-
      pose during the Spanish Civil War including Auden, who
      seemed to benefit from the experience. Abstracted in
      Dissertation Abstracts, 26 (October 1965), 2214-15. Re-
      vised and adapted in 1969.B5.

17   MAZZOCCO, ROBERT. "The Poet at Home." New York Review, 5
      (5 August), 5-7.
          After summarizing briefly Auden's poetic career,
      "polarities" of "the Just City and the False City, Eros
      and Agape, Kairos and Logos," Mazzocco describes About the
      House in some detail and concludes that it will not "ex-
      cite the young." Auden has "steadfastly avoided great-
      ness...."

18   MORGAN, KATHLEEN E. "The Analysis of Guilt: Poetry of
      W.H. Auden," in Christian Themes in Contemporary Poets.
      London: SCM Press, pp. 92-122.
          Concerns the later and "Christian phase" of Auden's
      work. Traces the evolution of his beliefs through a few
      of the earlier poems and then focuses on Auden's concepts
      of sin, salvation, love, faith, and man's being as ex-
      pressed in his later poems.

1965

19 PARKIN, REBECCA PRICE. "The Facsimile of Immediacy in
W.H. Auden's 'In Praise of Limestone.'" Texas Studies in
Literature and Language, 7 (Autumn), 295-304.
    Auden uses the devices of "informal conversation,"
"tenderness of tone," "paradoxes and riddles," and "con-
crete minutiae of daily life" to create the impression of
"direct immersion in reality." The landscape considered
negatively is a return to the womb, considered positively
a resurrection. Auden carefully prepares the reader to
think he is discovering truths on his own.

20 REPLOGLE, JUSTIN. "Auden's Intellectual Development 1950-
1960." Criticism, 7 (Summer), 250-62.
    Auden's last three volumes of verse (Nones, Shield of
Achilles and Homage to Clio) no longer grow out of an
"intellectual search" but out of "conclusions." Life is
"blessed" and the function of the poet is to "celebrate
this blessedness."

21 _____. "Auden's Marxism." PMLA, 80 (December), 584-95.
    Investigates Auden's verse and dramatic pieces to find
out his precise debt to Marx. Although Auden's "philosophical statements" from 1933 to 1938 are Marxist, Auden's
work is "not Marxist in any sense of the word."

22 ROBINSON, J.W. "W.H. Auden: Select Bibliography," in his
British Writers and Their Work. No. 5. Lincoln, Nebraska:
University of Nebraska, pp. 113-118.
    A revision and updating of the bibliography in earlier
editions of Hoggart's book. See 1957.A2 and 1965.B15.

23 RODWAY, ALLAN. "Logicless Grammar in Audenland." London
Magazine, n.s. 4 (March), 31-44.
    Auden adapts grammar to fit his metaphysical landscapes.
Logicless grammar is logical in a logicless land. Traces
the tendency of this habit in Auden's verse.

24 SCOTT, NATHAN A. "The Poetry of Auden," in his Four Ways of
Modern Poetry. Richmond: John Knox, pp. 71-92.
    Revised, shortened version of 1959.B6.

25 STANLEY, F.R. "Today the Struggle (A Critical Commentary on
Auden's Sonnet-sequence In Time of War)." Literary Half-
Yearly (Mysore), 6 (January), 74-88.
    Auden surveys human history from the standpoint of man's
choices, the limitations and responsibilities of his free-
dom, and the constant struggle for certainty. Not quite
a sonnet by sonnet account of In Time of War, Stanley's

essay nevertheless touches most of them and some of the verse Commentary accompanying the sonnets. The book was commissioned as a travel book, and thus "the emotional impulse...was...artificial." Its being a good commentary on man's wrong choices "is a happy accident."

26 WALLACE-CRABBE, CHRIS. "Auden Revisited." Dissent, 14 (Winter), 22-26.
    In reviewing Auden's career, finds two kinds of work. One is a body of verse which will continue to have historical interest for its perceptions of a period; the other is "a handful of poems" where Auden's "aesthetic and ethical concerns have found a temporary concord." Lists a few of these poems and examines "Prime" as different from most of the later poems. Believes the one consistent characteristic is that "his poetry asserts the uniqueness and restlessness of the individual spirit."

27 WEISSTEIN, ULRICH. "Sarastro's Brave New World or Die Zauberflote Transmogrified." Your Musical Cue (Indiana), 2 (December-January), 3-9.
    Additions of the sort Auden makes to Mozart's Die Zauberflote "are almost invariably in bad taste." Besides shifting the scenes, he turns the characters into analogues of the characters in The Tempest, bending them to a theme not Mozart's. His translation has a few beautiful passages, but mistranslations outnumber them.

28 WHITEHEAD, JOHN. "Auden: An Early Poetical Notebook." London Magazine, n.s. 5 (May), 85-91, 93, and plate facing p. 74.
    Describes the contents of an early notebook of Auden's containing prose pieces and one hundred and one poems, most of them unpublished. Discusses dating the poems and their relation to Auden's later work. Of those published later the copies have few variants. Quotes a number of the other pieces.

29 WICKES, GEORGE. "Interview with Christopher Isherwood." Shenandoah, 16 (Spring), 23-52.
    Questions Isherwood about his collaboration with Auden on plays and Journey to a War. Isherwood describes their meeting and subsequent friendship. See especially pp. 39-42.

30 WILLIAMS, MELVIN G. "Auden's 'Petition': A Synthesis of Criticism." The Personalist, 46 (Spring), 222-32.

1965

The poem "petition" serves as a general introduction to
Auden; for it contains most of the characteristics associated with his style: "the sense of the contemporary, ...
apparent ease of writing, ...obscurity." Williams examines
the poem closely, giving the readings of various critics
and his own view.

31 WOODHOUSE, A.S.P. "W.H. Auden," in The Poet and His Faith.
Chicago: University of Chicago Press, pp. 286-93.
Auden's spiritual journey contrasts to Eliot's in
length of duration and in the influences behind it. Pre-
monitions of Auden's direction appear in New Year Letter
and are realized in For the Time Being. Reprinted:
1966.B22.

32 WRIGHT, GEORGE T. "A General View of Auden's Poetry."
Tennessee Studies in Literature, 10, 43-64.
Surveys Auden's various techniques as a response to
those critics whose early predictions of Auden's success
were unfulfilled because he did not continue to write
either what they wanted or expected. Auden's subject
has always been the inner life of man, not society; the
outer world merely symbolizes the inner reality. Revised:
1969.A9.

1966 A BOOKS

1 BRUEHL, WILLIAM J. "The Auden/Isherwood Plays." Ph.D.
dissertation, University of Pennsylvania.
Attempts to ascertain the contributions of each, Auden
and Isherwood, to their plays and the respective influences of Eliot, Brecht, and Ibsen as well as those of
"popular theatre, music hall practice, and folk plays."
Also emphasizes a "psychological interpretation" over
social protest. Appends a verbatim transcript of a tele-
phone interview with Isherwood. Abstracted in Dissertation Abstracts, 27 (November 1966), 1931-A.

2 MORSE, DONALD E. "'Darning and the Eight-fifteen': Artistry
and Thought in W.H. Auden's 'For the Time Being.'" Ph.D.
dissertation, University of Connecticut.
Comments on the inadequacy of most Auden criticism;
describes the "subject and form" of "For the Time Being";
and discusses its technique and art." Abstracted in
Dissertation Abstracts, 27 (April 1967), 3465-A.

1966

3   PANAHI, M.M. "The Ethic of Love: The Philosophical Develop-
       ment of W.H. Auden's Poetry, 1922-1960." Ph.D. disserta-
       tion, University of Exeter.
          Outlines and explores the various stages in the develop-
       ment of Auden's idea of love by examining his underlying
       motives: "psychological, philosophical, religious, ethic-
       al, and political: From an interest in nature Auden moves
       through these stages to a concern with alienation in a
       world without religion or metaphysics.

4   PARK, LEA G. "Poet of Perspectives: The Style of W.H.
       Auden." Ph.D. dissertation, Northwestern University.
          Finds in Auden's verse a "metonymic perspective" and
       therefore, according to Roman Jakobson, a realistic world
       view and "a hostile relation to nature." Abstracted in
       Dissertation Abstracts, 27 (May 1967), 3967-A.

5   TWINING, EDWARD S. "Love and Politics in the Early Poetry
       of W.H. Auden." Ph.D. dissertation, University of
       Connecticut.
          Auden's political ideology is inseparable from his con-
       cept of "love," even in those poems which seem most to
       present political involvement. Discusses poems through
       1933. Abstracted in Dissertation Abstracts, 27 (June
       1967), 4268-A.

1966 B   SHORTER WRITINGS

1   BLOOM, ROBERT. "W.H. Auden's Bestiary of the Human." Vir-
       ginia Quarterly Review, 42 (Spring), 207-33.
          Explores the "animal-man contrast" in Auden's poems and
       shows the changes in Auden's use of this device over the
       years. These "animal" poems define Auden's idea of the
       human being and his attitudes towards mankind.

2   CALLAN, EDWARD. "Auden's Ironic Masquerade: Criticism as
       Morality Play." University of Toronto Quarterly, 35
       (January), 133-43.
          Analyzes The Sea and the Mirror part by part as repre-
       senting Auden's concern about the value of art and the
       values of his own work. The subject of Part I is the
       artist, of II the work of art, of III the audience. Re-
       lates, to a degree, this aesthetic criticism to The Dyer's
       Hand.

3   EHRENPREIS, IRVIN. "Poetry Without Despair." The Virginia
       Quarterly Review, 42 (Winter), 163-65.

1966

A short review that explains some of the Briticisms in About the House. "Geography," for example, "is a British euphemism for toilet."

4   FALCK, COLIN. "The Exposed Heart." Encounter, 27 (August), 77-83.
    Auden's theories about art are related to his theories about life ("Art is a second, escape world cut off from real life altogether") and the way to live. Auden develops "his own very personal answer to Romantic-Symbolism...."

5   FRASER, G.S. "Auden: In Memory of W.B. Yeats," in Master Poems of the English Language. Edited by Oscar Williams. New York: Trident Press, pp. 1017-21.
    In writing "In Memory of W.B. Yeats," Auden had to solve problems created by the English attitude towards Ireland in the thirties, an attitude partly of "boredom and irritation" and partly "one of profound historical guilt." Against the notions that Ireland is stuffy or crazy, that Yeats' assertions are ridiculous or "dangerous," that his way of life is like that "of a country curate purred at by genteel spinsters," Auden imparts "Yeats' superhuman mastery in the handling of words...." The poem asks us to respond to Yeats' music, "the magnificent noise," and not to judge the man or his message. Gives a close-reading analysis of the poem.

6   FRIEDMAN, S. "Auden and Hardy." Notes & Queries, n.s. 13 (November), 419.
    Finds the "inspiration" for Auden's ballad "Victor" in Hardy's "The Newcomer's Wife" and "At a Watering-Place."

7   HARRIS, HENRY. "The Symbol of the Frontier in the Social Allegory of the 'Thirties." Zeitschrift fur Anglistik und Amerikanistik, 14 (April), 127-40.
    The symbol of the frontier coupled with the allegory of the heroic quest is of frequent occurrence in the writers with Marxist leanings during the thirties, including Auden. Compares their uses "with traditional allegorical devices."

8   MacNEICE, LOUIS. The Strings Are False: An Unfinished Autobiography. New York: Oxford University Press, passim.
    Scattered comments on Auden, his beliefs, feelings, and ideas about life and art: "...you came away from his presence always encouraged; here at least was someone to

whom ideas were friendly...who would always have an interest in the world and always have something to say."

9   MITCHELL, BREON. "W.H. Auden and Christopher Isherwood: The
    'German Influence,'" Oxford German Studies, 1: 163-72.
        Contrary to the views of many critics, Auden was in-
    fluenced very little by either Brecht or Toller in his
    plays. Most of the influences derive from non-German
    sources like Ibsen, Shaw, Cocteau, Eliot, Hans Christian
    Anderson, Lewis Carroll, and English Christmas pantomine.
    German influences are limited to those of the cabaret and
    the political atmosphere during Auden's and Isherwood's
    visits in the thirties. An early manuscript version of
    The Dog Beneath the Skin shows us the "real" influences.

*10 MORTIMER, ANTHONY. "W.H. Auden," in Modern English Poets:
    Five Introductory Essays. Milan-Varese: Instituto Edi-
    toriale Cisalpine, pp. 115-42.
        Not seen. Reprinted 1968.B9.

11   MUSTE, JOHN M. "The Sky is Aflame," in his Say That We Saw
    Spain Die. Seattle: University of Washington Press, pp.
    34-59.
        Auden's "Spain" is "most successful" in its "half-
    ironic treatment of the past and his romantic evocation of
    the future"; less so in "delineation of the present."
    Auden was too unfamiliar with the struggle in Spain to
    verbalize it effectively. Discussion of Auden appears
    only on pp. 56-59.

12   PORTER, PETER. "The Assent of '36: An Encomium of Auden and
    MacNeice's 'Letter from Iceland.'" Ambit, 27: 18-23.
        Praise for the book Letters from Iceland as an enjoy-
    able travel book, "the most perfect anatomy of Britain in
    the Thirties," the final expression of "English literary
    confidence," some of the finest light verse written, a
    reminder of the pleasure to be derived from poetry. Porter
    comments on each part of the book, giving generous ex-
    amples from each.

13   REPLOGLE, JUSTIN. "Auden's Religious Leap." Wisconsin
    Studies in Contemporary Literature, 7 (Winter-Spring),
    47-75.
        Since Freud, Marx, and Kierkegaard are part of the same
    tradition, Auden's conversion to Christianity is a "move
    from one branch of post-Hegelian Germanic thought to an-
    other." Explores the Kierkegaardian thought in a few of
    Auden's poems, particularly "The Quest" and For the Time
    Being.

1966

14   ROSENHEIM, EDWARD W., JR.   "The Elegiac Act: Auden's 'In
     Memory of W.B. Yeats.'"   College English, 27 (February),
     422-25.
         Applies to Auden's poem the proposition that our knowl-
     edge of the poem's "historic identity" conditions the
     reader's response.   Sees the poem as "ritual exercise" im-
     pressive by its "virtuosity."

15   SCHORER, MARK.   "Auden: September 1, 1939," in Master Poems
     of the English Language.   Edited by Oscar Williams.   New
     York: Trident Press, pp. 1025-28.
         Auden's textual changes in different printings of this
     poem affect the meaning.   Special attention is given to
     stanza eight, omitted in the last printing of the poem.
     Auden's style imitates Yeats' colloquial style in "Easter
     1916"; his thought is set briefly against the historical
     backdrop of the German invasion of Poland and the coming
     war.

16   STONIER, G.W.   "New Poets," in Gog Magog.   Freeport, New York:
     Books for Libraries Press, pp. 171-76.
         Reprint of 1933.B3.

17   STRAVINSKY, IGOR AND ROBERT CRAFT.   Themes and Episodes.   New
     York: Alfred A. Knopf, passim.
         Presents an intimate view of Auden in many moods,
     offering opinions on practically everything.   Although
     accounts of Auden are throughout the book, they are easily
     found in the index, p.i.   Reprints 1964.B11 on pp. 51-54.

18   WEIMER, DAVID R.   "Rome Sacked," in his The City as Metaphor.
     New York: Random House, pp. 123-43.
         Describes the characteristic elements as well as vari-
     ations in Auden's use of the city as an image throughout
     his career.   In general the poet loves two cities and can
     neither reconcile them nor relinquish one.

19   WHEELER, CHARLES B.   The Design of Poetry.   New York: W.W.
     Norton, pp. 131-36.
         Analyzes Auden's sonnet "And the age ended, and its
     last deliverer died" to illustrate how to read an allegory
     that uses no personification.

20. WHITE, ERIC WALTER.   "The Rake's Progress," in his Stravinsky:
     The Composer and His Works.   London: Faber, pp. 412-28,
     493-94, passim.
         A bibliographical description of The Rake's Progress
     and an account of the inception of the idea and its growth

into an opera. Details the parts written by Kallman according to Stravinsky and Auden's manipulation and adaptations of Hogarth's material as well as, of course, a musical description of the opera. Discusses setting to music Auden's "Elegy for J.F.K." on pp. 493-94.

21 WHITEHEAD, LEE M. "Art as Communion: Auden's 'The Sea and the Mirror.'" Perspective, 14 (Spring), 171-78.
       Auden reminds us that the image seen in the mirror is the reverse of the real world. Thus "when art seems most escape, it leads most directly to commitment." We should, then, read the poem "backwards"; for "all values are reversed."

22 WOODHOUSE, A.S.P. "W.H. Auden: The Poet and His Faith." Midway, 7 (Winter), 50-57.
       Reprint of 1965.B31.

1967 A BOOKS

1 NELSON, GERALD B. "The Problem of Persona in the Poetry of W.H. Auden, 1940-1966." Ph.D. dissertation, Columbia University.
       Relates Auden's use of the persona to his personal problems, from his disillusionment with liberalism through the Kierkegaardian and Christian influences on him. Abstracted in Dissertation Abstracts, 29 (July 1968), 269-A. Revised and adapted: 1969.A4.

2 WALSH, WILLIAM F. "The Heel of Achilles: Dialectic in the Long Poems of W.H. Auden." Ph.D. dissertation, Columbia University.
       Auden's long poems derive their structure and organization from one or more dialectics: "New Year Letter" from the "dialectics of psychology and history"; "For the Time Being" from "religion and metaphysics"; "The Sea and the Mirror" from "poetry"; and The Age of Anxiety from "psychology and society." Abstracted in Dissertation Abstracts, 28 (June 1968), 5075-75-A.

3 WARREN, RAYMOND. Song for St. Cecilia's Day: An Inaugural Lecture Delivered Before the Queen's University of Belfast on 20th November 1967. Belfast: The Queen's University, 43 pp.
       On the occasion of Warren's receiving the University Chair in Musical Composition, Warren describes the process of composing a musical setting for Auden's poem. He gives

1967

a close reading of the poem as it relates to his decisions
about the music and comments from the musician's point of
view on Auden's assertions about art, language, and music.
Pp. 1–17 constitute the lecture, and pp. 18–43 the music.

1967 B SHORTER WRITINGS

1   BLOOM, ROBERT. "Auden's Essays at Man: Long Views in the
     Early Poetry." Shenandoah, 18 (Winter), 6–11.
         Auden has had one view in his long career despite having
     held "short views" from time to time: "He has meditated
     ...on the nature, attributes, limitations, propensities,
     and destiny of man." These meditations, according to
     Bloom, have all grown out of immediate concern in his own
     life and are "rarely undertaken for their own sake." The
     Auden we now know (in his work after 1940) was there to
     be known in the earliest years.

2   BRUEHL, WILLIAM J. "Polus Naufrangia: A Key Symbol in The
     Ascent of F6." Modern Drama, 10 (September), 161–64.
         Reveals the various levels at which the symbol, Polus
     Naufrangia (shipwrecked at the pole), functions in Auden's
     play. Finds a parallel between the action of the play and
     the plight of Ulysses in Canto XXVI of Dante's Inferno.

3   CALLAN, EDWARD. "Auden's Goodly Heritage." Shenandoah, 18
     (Winter), 56–68.
         Looks at Auden's career in poetry from the standpoint
     of his opposition to tyranny, for "he has sought to un-
     cover its germinating places in the inner nature of man
     and even in the hitherto sacrosanct artistic imagination."
     Considers extensively the volume About the House.

4   _____. "W.H. Auden: The Farming of a Verse." Southern
     Review, n.s. 2 (April), 341–56.
         Relates Auden's poetic practice to his ontological
     concerns: how to be when caught in the demands of both
     freedom and necessity. Offers a close-reading analysis
     of "In Memory of W.B. Yeats." Argues that for Auden the
     technical elements of his craft create opportunities ana-
     logous in real life to finding freedom within necessity.

5   CHATURVEDI, B.N. English Poetic Drama of the Twentieth Cen-
     tury. Givalios: Kitab Ghar, pp. 76–85.
         In addition to the influence of Eliot and Brecht, Auden
     utilizes leftist political ideology, psychology of Freud,
     Jung, and Groddeck, and concern with social disorders.
     Rupert Doone's "Group Theatre" influenced Auden along with

other young playwrights of the thirties, for it was their
"rallying ground." Generally Auden's plays lack single-
ness of purpose because he and Isherwood "tried to con-
dense too much into them...," and"...vacillated between
the propagandist attitude and the desire to justify the
use of poetry by indulging in pseudo-mysticism."

6 CONNORS, JAMES J. "Poets and Politics: A Study of the
Careers of C. Day Lewis, Stephen Spender and W.H. Auden in
the 1930's." Ph.D. dissertation, Yale University.
    Describes Oxford University of the 1920's and argues
that the later radicalism of Day Lewis, Spender, and
Auden derives from their experience as undergraduates.
Tries to define how each poet worked out his particular
political view. Abstracted in Dissertion Abstracts, 28
(April 1968), 4085-86-A.

7 DOBREE, BONAMY. "W.H. Auden." Shenandoah, 18 (Winter), 18-
22.
    An appreciation of a long acquaintance with Auden and
his verse. Says many of Auden's poems have "become part
of what I live by."

8 DODDS, E.R. "Background to a Poet: Memories of Birmingham."
Shenandoah, 18 (Winter), 6-11.
    Biographical essay putting Auden in the context of the
city in which he grew up. Relates Auden and his work to
the education and geography supplied him by Birmingham.

9 ELLMANN, RICHARD. "Gazebos and Gashouses," in his Eminent
Domain: Yeats Among Wilde, Joyce, Pound, Eliot, and
Auden. New York: Oxford University Press, 97-126,
passim.
    Treats modern poetry as a struggle for territory, of
poets' encroachment on one another's domains and making
them their own. Yeats is the central figure with whom
Auden and the other younger poets "conflict."

10 FITZGERALD, DAVID. "Auden's City." The Dublin Magazine, 6,
no. 2, 3-17.
    The idea of human community has always been present in
Auden's work, but only in the last fifteen years" (i.e.,
since the early 50's) has it found expression in the metaphor the "city."

11 FREMANTLE, ANNE. "Anima Naturaliter Christiana." Shenandoah,
18 (Winter), 69-77.

1967

> Sets forth the ingredients entering into Auden's Chris-
> tianity and his views of Christianity, the church, and the
> saints.

12   HOLLANDER, JOHN. "Auden at Sixty." Atlantic, 220 (July),
      84-87.
> A summary of Auden's career, which "has been full of
> the ambivalences and paradoxes that have marked the moral
> history of the past forty years." Auden's personality is
> described against the backdrop of his times.

13   IZZO, CARLO. "Goodbye to the Mezzogiorno." Shenandoah, 18
      (Winter), 80-82.
> A narration of the events leading up to the origin and
> writing of the poem "Goodbye to the Mezzogiorno," and
> ending with its publication in Italy in an Italian trans-
> lation by Carlo Izzo on facing pages.

14   KALLMAN, CHESTER. "Looking and Thinking Back." London Maga-
      zine, n.s. 6 (January), 80-82.
> Reprint of 1964.B11; 1966.B17.

15   LOWELL, ROBERT, et. al. "Five Tributes." Shenandoah, 18
      (Winter), 45-47.
> Appreciative comments and reminiscences an Auden's six-
> tieth birthday by Robert Lowell, Louise Bogan, M.F.K.
> Fisher, John Betjeman, and Leonard Bernstein.

16   MITCHISON, NAOMI. "Young Auden." Shenandoah, 18 (Winter),
      12-15.
> Reminiscence of Auden at the beginning of his career as
> a poet. Looks kindly at the young poet from an older
> poet's point of view.

17   MORSE, DONALD E. "The Nature of Man in Auden's 'For the Time
      Being.'" Renascence, 19 (Winter), 93-100.
> Auden believes man has a natural inclination to evil
> but through the Incarnation may do good. Traces the
> source of this belief in tradition and theological com-
> mentary and uses the belief in an interpretation of "For
> the Time Being."

18   _____. "'For the Time Being': Man's Response to the
      Incarnation." Renascence, 19 (Summer), 190-97.
> "For the Time Being" presents three possible responses
> to God, rejection, complete acceptance, and vacillation.
> These represent the choices of Herod, Simeon, and the
> chorus. Though Auden's view is not original, he asserts
> it "with clarity and precision."

19   PLATT, POLLY. "Interview: W.H. Auden." American Scholar,
      36 (Spring), 266-70.
          A personal narrative account of Auden in Austria with
      subjective descriptions of Auden along with Auden's com-
      ments on people, art and his current projects. Includes a
      sketch of Auden's house in Kirchstetten.

20   RIVERS, JAMES C.S. "Astronomy and Physics in British and
      American Poetry, 1920-1960." Ph.D. dissertation, Uni-
      versity of South Carolina.
          Examines Auden's use of astronomy and physics in "New
      Year Letter." Auden's poem is set against a backdrop of
      similar uses by poets like Donne, Noyes, MacLeish, and
      Jeffers. See pp. 217-26. Abstracted in Dissertation Ab-
      stracts, 28 (November 1967), 1826-A.

21   SALUS, PETER H. "Auden and Opera." The Quest (New York), 2
      (Spring), 7-14.
          Chronicles Auden's experiences with opera, describes
      characteristics of particular operas, and praises most of
      them.

22   SARANG, VILAS. "Personal Pronouns in the Poetry of W.H.
      Auden." Literary Criterion (Mysore), 7 (Summer), 51-63.
          Auden's poetry is rich in personal pronouns; which
      suggests that he is a social poet, but not the kind who
      wants a socialist revolution. A poet's use of personal
      pronouns reveals his attitudes towards himself and others,
      and Auden's poetry "is a poetry of the Persons." You is
      most used ("exploited"), I least used.

23   SELLERS, W.H. "New Light on Auden's The Orators." PMLA, 82
      (October), 455-64.
          Auden diagnoses the human condition in The Orators by "a
      series of discontinuous but not disconnected parables."
      Each of the first two books portray weak or neurotic men
      confronted by tests; the six odes of Book Three consider
      the general state "of England's health." Thinks The Ora-
      tors "the key to Auden's early work,."

24   SPEARS, MONROE K. "Auden and Dionysus." Shenandoah, 18
      (Winter), 85-95.
          Delineates the nature of the relationship of Auden's
      opera The Bassarids (with Chester Kallman) to Euripides'
      The Bacchae. Auden and Kallman "retain the principal
      characters and basic action...but reinterpret them in
      modern operatic terms...."

1967

25 SYMONS, JULIAN. "Early Auden." Shenandoah, 18 (Winter), 48-
    50.
        Claims a new voice for Auden in Look, Stranger! (The
    Double Man) and compares the Auden of 1967 with the Auden
    of 1937 when New Verse issued its Double Number on Auden.

26 TOLLEY, A.T. "The Printing of Auden's Poems (1928) and
    Spender's Nine Experiments." Library, 5th series, 22
    (June), 149-50.
        Questions Spender's statements about the sequence of
    events in the printing of Auden's poems and his own, as
    Spender apparently confuses some of the dates in his remi-
    niscences.

27 WERLICH, EGON. "W.H. Auden," in his Poetry Analysis. Dort-
    mund: Lambert Lensing, pp. 223-28.
        Analyzes first the persona of "Musee des Beaux Arts," a
    visitor in the Musee distinguished from "the connoisseur
    and the general public"; proceeds to structure as reflect-
    ing a process unfolding or a development, "...his under-
    standing increases of what he first only generally calls
    the 'human position' of suffering"; then elucidates the
    imagery juxtaposing the sufferers with the indifferent;
    and finally explores the reactions of a reader, who has
    been "drawn...into a fresh encounter with the human world
    in which he actually lives."

1968 A BOOKS

1   ARNOLD, LESLIE E. "The Motif of the 'Quest' in the Early
    Works of W.H. Auden." Ph.D. dissertation, Simon Fraser
    University.
        Contends that the "Quest" is the sole unifying image of
    Auden's early work, the concept that a person must make his
    own order in a chaotic and decadent world. Defines the
    nature of this motif and traces Auden's use of it in the
    early poems and the plays. Relates it to Auden's personal
    search for identity.

2   BELL, I.M. "From Myth to Allegory: A Study of the Poetry of
    W.H. Auden with Special Reference to the Poet's Intention."
    Ph.D. dissertation, Rhodes University, South Africa.
        Studies in detail the mythology Auden developed in
    early works like Paid on Both Sides and The Orators and its
    significance for the allegorical aspect of later works.

*3   DAVIDSON, EDWARD J. "W.H. Auden's 'New Year Letter' and Its
       Relationship to the Rest of His Work." Ph.D. dissertation,
       University of London (Berkbeck College).
          Not seen. Cited in 1972.A2.

4   GREENBERG, HERBERT. Quest for the Necessary: W.H. Auden and
       the Dilemma of Divided Consciousness. Cambridge: Harvard
       University Press, 209 pp.
          Contains prefatory note by Stephen Spender. For Auden
       the way to live is the way to love, and the obstacle con-
       fronting proper love is the divided consciousness. Thus
       all Auden's work aims at defining the concept of love and
       resolving the problem of a divided consciousness. Green-
       berg attempts to explain the apparent vacillation, con-
       tradiction, and frequent shifts in position noted by other
       critics through this focus on love as Auden's central con-
       cern.

5   SPEARS, MONROE K. The Poetry of W.H. Auden: The Disenchanted
       Island. New York: Galaxy Books.
          Reprint of 1963.A2. Corrected impression with new
       preface.

6   WOODBERY, POTTER. Redeeming the Time: The Theological Argu-
       ment of Auden's "For the Time Being." School of Arts and
       Sciences Research Papers, No. 18. Atlanta: Georgia State
       College, 41 pp.
          Attempts to provide a frame of reference to explain
       "For the Time Being," Auden's "most explicit poetic state-
       ment" of his religious beliefs. Arranges the discussion
       under the headings of Ideas and Poverty; Depravity; The
       Wrath of God; The Incarnation; and Redeeming the Time.

1968 B   SHORTER WRITINGS

1   ARMYTAGE, W.H.G. "The Disenchanted Mecanophobes in Twentieth
       Century England." Extrapolation, 9 (May), 33-60.
          Auden plays a very small part in this essay, merely pp.
       47-48; mentioned is his disenchantment with the machine
       age ("the third great disappointment") and the influence
       on him of Charles Williams.

2   BARNES, T.R. Poetry Appreciation. London: Faber, pp. 24-35.
          Discusses the relationship of the poetic technique to
       meaning in two poems. "Mundus et Infans" and "On This
       Island."

3   BLOOM, ROBERT.   "The Humanization of Auden's Early Style."
     PMLA, 83 (May), 443-54.
          Auden changes from an elliptical style in his earliest
     poems to a "rhetorical" style about 1940; this shift marks
     "a humanization of his style," an effort to bring his
     poetry closer to "particularized human experience." Takes
     up Jarrell's argument (1941.B5) point by point and tries
     to answer the charges there by arguing that Auden's shifts
     occur out of a "growing humanity."

4   FAIRCHILD, HOXIE NEALE.   Religious Trends in English Poetry.
     Vol. 6. New York: Columbia University Press, pp. 134-
     144, 229-301, 443-45, passim.
          Believes the influence of the Spanish Civil War on
     Auden, or on any other "poet of talent," a very slight one.
     Discusses Auden's view of man as influenced by Williams
     and Catholicism. Also surveys Auden's religious beliefs
     from his early years to his "conversion" and relates them
     to the times. See the "Index of Names" for the numerous
     passages about Auden.

5   JURAK, MIRKO.   "English Political Verse Drama of the Thirties:
     Revision and Alteration." Acta Neophilologica (Ljubljana),
     1: 67-78.
          Shows the variations between the published texts and
     the performances of The Dance of Death, The Dog Beneath the
     Skin, The Ascent of F6, and On the Frontier. These changes
     came either from the author or the director during prepa-
     rations of the play for production or from the censor.
     They also in Jurak's opinion affected the reception of
     some of the plays and even caused some confusion and error
     in reviews and criticisms of the plays. Three different
     versions, for example, exist as texts for The Ascent of F6.
     Some changes, of course, improved the plays.

6   LEWARS, KENNETH.   "Auden's Swarthmore Chart." Connecticut
     Review, 1 (April), 44-56.
          An account, with a facsimile, of a chart of human experi-
     ence Auden prepared in 1943, "a graphic representation of
     his characteristic thinking in the early forties." Relates
     the chart to Auden's beliefs and to "The Sea and the Mir-
     ror" which Auden was working on at that time.

7   MENDELSON, EDWARD.   "The Coherence of Auden's The Orators."
     English Literary History, 35: 114-33.
          Uses the "absurd command," like the call of God to an
     Apostle, the creation of order from outside man, as a
     theme to "unravel...theme and structure" in The Orators.

The three Books of The Orators are framed by a "Prologue"
and "Epilogue," the contrast between which clarifies the
coherence of the entire work. The "Prologue" portrays
failure, restated variously in the body of the work; the
"Epilogue" affirms "the absurd and positive image of
divine success."

8   MORAES, DOM. My Son's Father. London: Secker & Warburg, pp.
     190-92, 205-206.
        Brief episode wherein Moraes recounts how Auden as Pro-
     fessor of Poetry helped him with his verse at Oxford.
     Describes Auden from the point of view of an undergraduate
     approaching his boyhood idol.

9   MORTIMER, ANTHONY. "W.H. Auden," in his Modern English Poets:
     Seven Introductory Essays. Toronto: Forum House, pp.
     113-40.
        Reprint of 1966.B10.

10   ORWELL, GEORGE. The Collected Essays, Journalism and Letters
     of George Orwell. Edited by Sonia Orwell and Ian Angus.
     New York: Harcourt, Brace & World, Inc., pp. 493-527.
        Reprint of 1940.B6.

11   PRYCE-JONES, DAVID. "Conversation with W.H. Auden." Daily
     Telegraph Magazine, 201 (9 August), 22.
        Visit to Auden in Kirchstetten, Austria. Describes
     Auden's physical appearance and his surroundings and lists
     some of his opinions about the famous ("Yeats and Robert
     Frost were...'horrid'"), about work ("I've always been
     puritanical about work"), about his revisions and his re-
     jections of his old poems ("It's my privilege to revise"),
     and England ("England has become vulgar and unconsciously
     provincial"). Reprinted 1969.B13.

12   SPEARS, MONROE K. "Auden's Longer Poems," in Modern Poetry:
     Essays in Criticism. Edited by John Hollander. New York:
     Oxford University Press, pp. 359-94.
        Reprinted from 1963.A2, Chapter III.

13   STEAD, C.K. "Auden's 'Spain.'" London Magazine, n.s. 7
     (March), 41-54.
        Outlines the structure of "Spain," reviews Auden's ex-
     perience in Spain according to the "gossip." Replies to
     various criticisms (dishonesty; detachment), and explores
     the relationship of public expression and private feeling
     in Auden.

1968

14 TOLLEY, A.T. "The Thirties Poets at Oxford." University of
    Toronto Quarterly, 37 (July), 338-58.
        Examines the work and relationships as undergraduates
    of Auden, Day Lewis, Spender, and MacNeice. Section IV
    treats Auden specifically, describing generally the tenor
    of the poems appearing in Public School Verse, Oxford
    Poetry, and others. Believes Eliot "was an example rather
    than a model" for the younger poets, showing them the
    possibilities for poetry in contemporary material.

15 VALGEMAE, MARDI. "Auden's Collaboration with Isherwood on
    The Dog beneath the Skin." Huntington Library Quarterly,
    31 (August), 373-83.
        Talks with Isherwood, copies of letters and scenarios,
    and carbon copies of two manuscripts of early versions help
    to illuminate the question of joint authorship of The Dog
    Beneath the Skin. Detailed examination of these resources
    shows the work to be "a genuine collaboration."

16 WEINTRAUB, STANLEY. "The Committed Noncombatants," in his
    The Last Great Cause. New York: Weybright & Talley, pp.
    54-87.
        Includes an account of Auden in Spain (pp. 65-71) along
    with other writers who seem to have been influenced by the
    Civil War whether they went or not. Some of the images
    and "Shakespearian-sounding lines in "Spain" may have
    come from a relief map of Spain in the main square of
    Valencia. By his poem, Auden did "his proper job." See
    index (p. 332) for additional brief comments on Auden.

17 WESTLAKE, JOHN H.J. "W.H. Auden's 'The Shield of Achilles':
    An Interpretation." Literatur in Wissenschaft und Unter-
    richt (Kiel), 1: 50-57.
        Auden's The Shield of Achilles contrasts the classical
    and modern attitudes; "war is no longer a heroic activity
    ...but rather a denial of Man's humanity and individuality."
    Westlake shows step by step in the structure, in the im-
    ages, and in the classical and Christian parallels the
    working out of this theme.

18 WILLIAMS, RAYMOND. "Auden and Isherwood," in his Drama from
    Ibsen to Brecht. London: Chatto & Windus, pp. 199-206.
        Revised edition of 1952.B12. Revisions are mostly in
    wording.

W. H. Auden: A Reference Guide

1969

1969 A   BOOKS

1   BOYER, ROBERT H.   "Anglo-Saxon and Middle English Influences
in the Poetry of W.H. Auden."   Ph.D. dissertation, University of Pennsylvania.
    Studies the biographical, technical, and thematic bases
of Auden's "Anglo-Saxon voice."   Auden's most "successful
and original" poems derive from the influence of the older
verse.   Abstracted in Dissertation Abstracts International,
31 (September 1970), 1262-63-A.

2   CLARK, VERA F.W.   "The Rhetoric of W.H. Auden's Verse Plays."
Ph.D. dissertation, University of Washington.
    Studies four of Auden's verse plays (Paid on Both Sides,
The Dance of Death, For the Time Being, and "The Sea and
the Mirror") to find the "message" through his rhetorical
devices.   Abstracted in Dissertation Abstracts International, 30 (December 1969), 2651-A.

3   MENDELSON, EDWARD.   "Auden's Landscape."   Ph.D. dissertation,
Johns Hopkins University.
    Auden uses landscape as metaphor and analogy; these
uses relate to his poetic voices, which in turn reveal, or
are part of, his "modes of perception."   Discusses also
the theme of the quest and Auden's view of time and eter-
nity.

4   NELSON, GERALD.   Changes of Heart: A Study of the Poetry of
W.H. Auden.   Perspectives in Criticism, no. 21.   Berkeley:
University of California Press, 175 pp.
    Contains bibliography of Auden's works and lists about
fifty critical items about Auden.   Analyzes poems by
focusing a "persona" and the dramatic pieces by focusing
a "mask."   Considers the poems, etc., chronologically so
as to display "evidence of development and direction in
Auden's work."   The early persona is the petitioner or
questor; the later persona is one whose petitions and
questions have either been answered or considered foolish.
Revises and adapts 1967.A1.

5   REPLOGLE, JUSTIN.   Auden's Poetry.   Seattle: University of
Washington Press, 558 pp.
    Reworks some of the ideas in Replogle's articles al-
ready listed.   Discusses Auden's poems as "a storehouse
of ideas, as the dwelling place of speakers, and...as a
verbal contraption."   The first three chapters take up
these divisions as subjects and a fourth, on comedy, offers
Replogle's conclusions.   In general and in some particular

93

poems, treats Auden's work from the standpoint of his style.

*6 SARANG, VILAS. "The Verbal Contraption: Technique and Style in the Poetry of W.H. Auden." Ph.D. dissertation, University of Bombay.
Not seen. Cited in 1972.A2.

7 STIEHL, HARRY C., JR. "Auden's Artists: Portraits of the Artist in the Poetry of W.H. Auden." Ph.D dissertation, University of Texas at Austin.
Auden's poetic portraits of other artists illustrate his "periods" and development. Assesses also the influence of these poems on similar poems by other modern poets. Abstracted in <u>Dissertation Abstracts International</u>, 30 (October 1969), 1576-77-A.

8 THORNBURG, THOMAS R. <u>Prospero, the Magician Artist</u>: <u>Auden's The Sea and the MIrror</u>. Ball State Monograph Number Fifteen. Muncie, Indiana: Ball State University, 35 pp.
Believes Auden's Prospero is a figure of the "failed artist, indeed, representing Auden himself...." and that <u>The Sea and the Mirror</u> is "an artistic presentation: of Auden's aesthetic theories. Art is the mirror which reflects the condition of life around us, and Auden tells us that we should not mistake the artist for a magician, nor art for magic.

9 WRIGHT, GEORGE T. <u>W.H. Auden</u>. Twayne United States Authors Series, 144. New York: Twayne Publishers, 180 pp.
Sees Auden's development as consistent and treats his works historically, thereby revealing their unity. Offers a general view of Auden and his works rather than an extended analysis of any particular poems. Contains a brief annotated bibliography. Reprints 1965.B32 in somewhat revised form.

1969 B SHORTER WRITINGS

1 HAMPSHIRE, STUART. "W.H. Auden," in his <u>Modern Writers and Other Essays</u>. London: Chatto & Windus, pp. 19-29.
A general discussion and assessment of Auden's achievement, examining his virtuosity of technique, his irreverence, his didacticism, and his later "gentlemanly" restraint. Auden is, "and will surely remain, one of the most quotable of poets...." American edition: 1970.B8.

2   HARDY, BARBARA.   "W.H. Auden, Thirties to Sixties: A Face
     and a Map." Southern Review, n.s. 5 (Summer), 655-72.
          Explores the public and private aspects of Auden's
     work. His poems move both ways, sometimes enlarging a
     private feeling and sometimes brings the public world into
     the private. Discusses a number of poems which illustrate
     this characteristics of Auden.

3   HAZARD, FORREST E. "The Father Christmas Passage in Auden's
     'Paid on Both Sides.'" Modern Drama, 12 (September), 155-
     64.
          Defines the dramatic function of the Father Christmas
     passage as representing the "call" in "the traditional
     quest pattern" and argues that Auden reworked the details
     of the traditional mummer's play to emphasize relevance
     to modern times. The passage is a "warning dream" offer-
     ing moral guidance to the hero.

4   HOLLOWAY, JOHN. "The Master as Joker." Art International,
     13 (January), 17-20.
          Compares Auden's poems to expressionist paintings, for
     they create their effects by "parataxis," adding item by
     item in "simple juxtaposition." Also points out differ-
     ences between Auden's technique and Eliot's and argues
     that it is a mistake to want Auden to be another Eliot.
     Auden "registers the civilization of our century more
     comprehensively than any other poet who has written in
     English."

5   HOSKINS, KATHARINE BAIL. Today the Struggle. Austin: Uni-
     versity of Texas Press, pp. 165-82, 207-218, passim.
          A general discussion of Auden's work in the thirties.
     Discusses Auden's early plays as representative of his
     political concerns before he went to Spain and then On the
     Frontier, "a final gesture for the Popular Front before
     the authors resigned in despair." Although a good part of
     Auden's writing at this time (1936-39) is topical and very
     close to propaganda, it has been "much less susceptible"
     to historical circumstances than that of some others.
     Revises and adapts 1965.B16.

6   JARRELL, RANDALL. Third Book of Criticism. New York: Far-
     rar, Straus & Giroux, pp. 115-50.
          Reprints: 1941.B5; 1945.B5.

7   JURAK, MIRKO. "The Group Theatre: Its Development and Sig-
     nificance for the Modern English Theatre." Acta Neophilo-
     logica. 2: 3-43.

"Detailed history of the Group Theatre; footnotes lists reviews of the productions." Not seen. Cited in 1972.A2.

8 LEHMANN, JOHN. In My Own Time. Boston: Little, Brown, Passim.
    Combines the two previous volumes of Lehmann's autobiography along with a third The Ample Proposition (1966). See 1955.B6.

9 MacNEICE, LOUIS. Modern Poetry. New York: Oxford Press, passim.
    Reprint of 1938.B10.

10 MANDLE, W.F. "Auden and the Failure of the Left." ANU Historical Journal, 6 (November), 3-9.
    Auden is a symbol of the failure of the Left in the thirties; he recognized it in 1938 when he left Europe. Like the Left, Auden was too ambivalent, too unsure of his role. Although "a superb social commentator and analyst...his ambivalence continually intrudes."

11 MAXWELL, D.E.S. "W.H. Auden: The Island and the City," in his Poets of the Thirties. London: Routledge & Kegan Paul, pp. 127-72.
    Describes four poems originally published in New Country, edited by Michael Roberts (1932), as having "quite openly a left-wing set." Revisions for their reprinting in Look, Stranger! signify very little change in Auden's ideas from the time of writing. Softens some of the harsh criticism of J.W. Beach's The Making of the Auden Canon by pointing out inconsistencies in the application of Beach's theory. Surveys various sorts of revisions as they relate to Marxian attitudes and discusses the growth of the images of city and island in Auden's work.

12 PRESS, JOHN. "W.H. Auden," in A Map of English Verse. London: Oxford University Press, pp. 186-98.
    Supplies source-book information about Auden: brief commentaries on Auden's reputation, his education, his reading, his Marxism, his expatriation, his Christianity, and his interest in music. Includes a dozen samples of Auden's criticism, five pages of Auden's verse, and a "select" bibliography.

13 PRYCE-JONES, DAVID. "Conversation with W.H. Auden." Holiday, 45 (June), 56, 66-67.
    Reprint of 1968.B11.

14   REEVES, JAMES, ed. "W.H. Auden," in his The Poets and Their
      Critics: Arnold to Auden. Vol. 3. London: Hutchinson,
      pp. 242-73.
          Collects excerpts from the critical commentary of thirty
      years to illustrate the widely divergent views on Auden.
      A brief introduction summarizes those views, and the first
      few pages reprint excerpts of Auden's opinions about poet-
      ry.

15   SAVAGE, D.S. "The Strange Case of W.H. Auden," in his The
      Personal Principle. Folcroft, Pennsylvania: The Folcroft
      Press, pp. 155-82.
          Reprint of 1944.B5.

16   STRAVINSKY, IGOR, AND ROBERT CRAFT. "From the Diaries of
      Robert Craft, 1948-1968." in their Retrospectives and Con-
      clusions. New York: Alfred A. Knopf, pp. 145-49, 160-65,
      173-79.
          Subjective account of Auden's acquaintance with Strav-
      insky and his circle of friends; anecdotes of Auden's re-
      actions and opinions appear throughout, his shock at the
      bawdiness of Pal Joey, for example.

1970 A BOOKS

1   BAHLKE, GEORGE W. The Later Auden: From "New Year Letter"
      to About the House. Literature in Perspective. New
      Brunswick, New Jersey: Rutgers University Press, 208 pp.
          Attempts to elucidate Auden's later poetry and refute
      the charges that his "vision is frivolous or ephemeral."
      Focuses on "New Year Letter," "The Sea and the Mirror,"
      "For the Time Being," and The Age of Anxiety, and the four
      volumes of poetry published in the fifties and sixties.
      Outlines Auden's "relation to Christian thought and...his
      understanding of it"; his return to Christianity as ex-
      pressed in "New Year Letter"; his "understanding of the
      relationship between literature and life" and between man
      and God; and in the concluding chapter "the dominant con-
      cerns and mode" of Auden's poetry from Nones to About the
      House. Reprints revised parts of 1960.A1.

2   BROPHY, JAMES D. W.H. Auden. Columbia Essays on Modern
      Writers, 54. New York: Columbia University Press, 48 pp.
          A general introduction to Auden and survey of his
      career, considered from the standpoint of Auden as "es-
      sentially a poet of the reasonable." Concludes with the
      difficulty of classifying Auden, although we may list his
      "salient characteristics."

1970

3   BUELL, FREDERICK H. "The Political Voice of W.H. Auden."
Ph.D. dissertation, Cornell University.
    Background and biographical study of Auden's political
orientation as it changes and as his work develops towards
"a thoroughly public verse." Abstracted in Dissertation
Abstracts International, 31 (June 1971), 6592-A.

4   DAVISON, DENNIS. W.H. Auden. Literature in Perspective.
London: Evans Brothers, 176 pp.
    Finds Auden's distinction in his "unpredictability."
He has made a sort of literary biography in keeping with
the aim of the series of relating the man to his writing.
Concludes with two letters by men who knew Auden well in
response to Davison's request "to evaluate the 'later
Auden.'" The analyses of the poems are both about Auden
and about the poems.

5   FULLER, JOHN. A Reader's Guide to W.H. Auden. London:
Thames & Hudson; New York: Farrar, Straus & Giroux, 288 pp.
    A commentary on Auden's poetry and drama in chronologic-
al sequence. Attempts explication of difficult passages
and traces sources and allusions. Arranged to be read
with Collected Shorter Poems (1966) and Collected Longer
Poems (1968). Contains biographical information, a brief
bibliography of biography and criticism, and an index of
poems (titles and first lines). Chapter 14 comments upon
"Some Poems Outside the Canon."

*6   QUESENBERY, WILLIAM D., JR. "Variant Readings in W.H. Auden's
Poetry: Collected Shorter Poems 1927-1957 and Collected
Longer Poems." Ph.D. dissertation, Columbia University.
Not seen. Cited in 1972.A2.

7   STOLL, JOHN E. W.H. Auden: A Reading. Ball State Monograph
Number Eighteen. Muncie, Indiana: Ball State University,
40 pp.
    Takes as his subject Auden's psychological duality and
its relation to his work and religious views. Auden believes modern man can either accept the condition of iso-
lation from the outer world, can "lobotomize himself through
self-evasion," or pursue human completeness and wholeness
"through Vision."

1970 B SHORTER WRITINGS

1   ANON. "Craft Interview--W.H. Auden." New York Quarterly, 1
(Winter), 7-13.

This interview is taken from a series of separate meetings with Auden in November 1969. Auden answers questions
about his technique ("I have two things working--some kind
of theme, and certain formal problems, metrical structure,
diction"); about his numerous revisions ("But the poems I
decided were unauthentic went out"); about reviews of his
work ("...my only complaint when I am reviewed is the
critic's lack of knowledge"); and about his opinions of the
contemporary literary scene.

2   BLOOM, ROBERT. "Poetry's Auden." Journal of Modern Litera-
     ture, I (first issue), 119-22.
          Review of Greenberg's Quest for the Necessary. Comments
     on Auden's contentment and mildness in his last years and
     goes on to review Greenberg's Quest for the Necessary (1968)
     as a "superb" book and compares it to Replogle's Auden's
     Poetry (1969).

3   BOGAN, LOUISE. "W.H. Auden," in her A Poet's Alphabet. New
     York: McGraw-Hill, pp. 30-50.
          Brings together Bogan's reviews of Auden from 1935 to
     1960, making a survey of one reviewer's attitudes over the
     years. Considers Auden as editor and essayist as well as
     poet. Reprints in separate parts the piece entitled "The
     Quest of W.H. Auden," in her Selected Criticism (New York:
     Noonday Press, 1966), pp. 275-88.

4   BOWEN, C. "Pardon for Writing Well." Poetry Magazine (Syd-
     ney), 18 (June), 3-12.
          Discusses the style and preferences of recent criticism
     and its general failure with Auden's work. Criticizes
     critics for devoting too much attention to Auden's changes,
     both the revisions of his work and in his thinking: his
     "changes are changes in the explication of constant atti-
     tudes." Praises City Without Walls for its "relaxed and
     objective" wisdom.

5   CALLAN, EDWARD. "W.H. Auden: Annotated Checklist II (1958-
     1969)." Twentieth Century Literature, 16 (January), 27-56.
          Continues 1958.B2, extending the number of items to 501.
     Notes the revised editions of major works and reissues of
     early works in new format. Retains the method of the ear-
     lier checklist and attempts "to make the list of essays
     and reviews as complete as possible and also to identify
     the contents of each."

6   EAGLETON, TERRY. "A Note on Auden," in Exiles and Emigres:
     Studies in Modern Literature. New York: Shocken Books,
     179-90.

1970

The motif expressed in Auden's early poem "Musee des Beaux Arts," that "normal" life goes on in the midst of or all around the extraordinary event, continues as a pattern through all his early work. This technique of presenting complete vision, however, remains only a technique. At Auden's worst it is parody--"mechanical combination of trivialising particular and glib generalisation." At his best, although he could overcome his glibness, he never quite achieved "totalisation."

7   FAULKNER, PETER. "Auden as Scrutineer." Durham University Journal, 32 (December), 56-60.
        Auden's reviews, published in the early numbers of Scrutiny "reveal some of Auden's preoccupations, and doubts, at the beginning of his career." These cover subjects ranging from education to Winston Churchill to Forster's life of Lowes Dickinson. Attempts to compare some of the opinions expressed there to those in Auden's early verse.

8   FULLER, ROY. Owls and Artificers. London: Andre Deutsch, passim.
        Auden has learned from Marianne Moore the uses of syllabic verse. Commentary on "Consider" appears on pp. 94-95.

9   HAMPSHIRE, STUART N. "W.H. Auden," in his Modern Writers and Other Essays. New York: Knopf, pp. 19-29. American edition of 1969.B1.

10   HAWORTH, HELEN E. "Man's Tragic Dilemma in Auden and Sophocles." Queen's Quarterly, 77 (Winter), 566-76.
        If, like Sophocles, Auden believes the best for man is not to have been born; he believes man's second best is acceptance of life, for man by "so doing asserts his authority over it."

*11 HAZARD, FORREST E. "The Ascent of F6: A New Interpretation." Times Literary Supplement (London), 15, 165-75.
        Not seen. Not in 1970 Times Literary Supplement. Cited in Journal of Modern Literature, 3 (February 1974), 534.

12   HOGGART, RICHARD. "The Long Walk: The Poetry of W.H. Auden," in his Speaking to Each Other. Vol. 2 London: Chatto & Windus, pp. 56-94.
        Reprint of the text of 1965.B15.

13   IRWIN, JOHN T. "MacNeice, Auden, and the Art Ballad." Con-
       temporary Literature, 11 (Winter), 58-79.
            Shows that Auden's references to St. James' Infirmary
       and "Frankie and Johnny" as "tunes" for "Miss Gee" and
       "Victor" indicate "general allusive background" rather than
       the actual tunes.

14   KERMODE, FRANK. "The Poet in Praise of Limestone." Atlantic,
       225 (May), 67-71.
            Relates Auden to the twentieth century by invoking the
       names of Tennyson and Dryden for parallels. "What we hear
       in the voice is a life; in the face we may even see an
       analogue of that limestone landscape...we grew up with."
       Views Auden as "a twentieth century institution."

15   LEITHAUSER, GLADYS GARNER. "W.H. Auden's 'Meiosis.'" English
       Language Notes, 8 (December), 126.
            Applies the biological meaning of meiosis, a kind of
       cell division, to a reading of Auden's poem.

16   MATERER, TIMOTHY. "Merton and Auden." Commonweal, 91 (27
       February), 577-80.
            Auden and Merton set "the borders of religious poetry."
       Though different in their attitudes, "their approaches to
       God are finally compatible." Explores the notion of two
       temperaments, the poet and antipoet, in each. Merton ex-
       presses "the heights of religious experience," Auden
       "remains on the level plains of Christian experience."

17   MORSE, DONALD E. "Meaning of Time in Auden's For The Time
       Being." Renascence, 22 (Spring), 162-68.
            Man need not consider time either linear or cyclical but
       "redeemed." Urges this view for an understanding of Auden's
       Oratorio.

18   _____. "Two Major Revisions in Auden's 'For the Time
       Being.'" English Language Notes, 7 (June), 294-97.
            Auden's revision in "The Meditation of Simeon" intends
       "to juxtapose two different--even conflicting--responses
       to divine revelation." The revision in the Narrator's last
       speech is for clarity.

19   NATTERSTAD, J.H. "Auden's 'It's No Use Raising a Shout': A
       New Perspective." Concerning Poetry, 3 (Spring), 17-20.
            The images of evolutionary biology along with the bird
       image suggests that man has "left behind" along with more
       obvious physical things his "religious certainty" and has
       little or no hope of "reestablishing ties...human or spiri-
       tual." Thus is built the note of despair.

1970

20   SCHWARTZ, DELMORE. Selected Essays of Delmore Schwartz.
        Edited by Donald Dike and David H. Zuckler. Chicago: Uni-
        versity of Chicago Press, pp. 143-52.
           Reprint of 1939.B12.

21   SMITH, ELTON EDWARD. "Member of the Group," in his Louis
        MacNeice. New York: Twayne Publishers, pp. 42-73, passim.
           About MacNeice, of course, but contains biographical
        information about Auden and his influence on and friendship
        with MacNeice.

22   SPEARS, MONROE K. "The Nature of Modernism: The City," in
        Dionysus and the City. New York: Oxford University Press,
        pp. 82-90.
           Auden has used the city as a principal image and symbol
        from his earliest poetry and later in his critical prose
        as well. Usually it is a symbol of civilization and re-
        sponsibility as opposed to lonely islands and sentimental
        escapism. Auden repeatedly in various ways admonished us
        to rebuild our cities. Included is commentary on this
        theme relating to The Bassarids, written with Chester Kall-
        man.

23   SPENDER, STEPHEN. "W.H. Auden and the Poets of the Thirties."
        in his Poetry Since 1939. Folcroft, Pennsylvania: Fol-
        croft Press.
           Reprint of 1946.B5.

24   STRAVINSKY, IGOR. "A Maker of Libretti." Harper's Magazine,
        240 (April), 112-14.
           Chatty account of two evenings with Auden in New York.
        Discussion of the arts, the "generation gap," and differ-
        ences the librettist must note between music and poetry.

25   THORNBURG, THOMAS R. "The Man with the Hatchet: Shapiro on
        Auden." Ball State University Forum, 11 (Summer), 25-34.
           Asserts that Shapiro's criticism of Auden is nonsense
        and replies to it point by point.

26   WEISSTEIN, ULRICH. "Reflections on a Golden Style: W.H.
        Auden's Theory of Opera." Comparative Literature, 22
        (Spring), 108-24.
           Surveys Auden's association with "a number of musical
        ventures," an area relatively neglected by literary schol-
        ars, and tries to define Auden's particular interest in
        music drama, relating it to his total "esthetic universe."

W. H. Auden: A Reference Guide

27   WHITE, ERIC WALTER. Benjamin Britten: His Life and Operas.
       Berkeley: University of California Press, pp. 22-27, 95-99.
       New edition of 1949.B14. Adds note on Auden's inten-
       tions in Paul Bunyan.

1971 A BOOKS

1   BYER, JAMES EDWIN. "The Literary Criticism of W.H. Auden
       Theory and Practice." Ph.D. dissertation, Duke University.
       Relates Auden's critical opinions to his attitudes
       toward psychology, politics, and religion. Places Auden's
       "practical" criticism in categories of "psychological,
       mythological, historical and sociological." Abstracted in
       Dissertation Abstracts International, 32 (March 1972),
       5221-22-A.

2   LEVITIN, ALEXIS A. "A Study in Revision: W.H. Auden's 'A
       Voyage' and 'Sonnets from China.'" Ph.D dissertation,
       Columbia University.
       Auden has revised these poems away from the "romantical-
       ly abstract and general" towards the "concrete and par-
       ticular." Studies these revisions in detail. Abstracted
       in Dissertation Abstracts International, 35 (January 1975),
       4532-33-A.

3   SCARFE, FRANCIS. W.H. Auden. Contemporary British Poets.
       Folcroft, Pennsylvania: Folcroft Press, 68 pp.
       Reprint of 1949.A1.

4   WHEELER, EDD DUDLEY. "W.H. Auden and His American Experience."
       Ph.D. dissertation, Emory University.
       Studies Auden's responses to the United States as
       represented in his work, both poetry and criticism. Chap-
       ter Three analyzes the libretto of Paul Bunyan. Abstracted
       in Dissertation Abstracts International, 32 (October 1971),
       2108-A.

1971 B SHORTER WRITINGS

1.   BLOODGOOD, JANE C. "The Ode in the Poetry of W.H. Auden and
       Stephen Spender." Ph.D. dissertation, The University of
       Tulsa.
       Argues that Auden is an "odic bard" and Spender is not.
       Measures Auden's and Spender's performance in this form
       against their aesthetic theories. Abstracted in Disserta-
       tion Abstracts International, 32 (September 1971), 1465-A.

1971

2   BROOKS, CLEANTH. A Shaping Joy: Studies in the Writer's
     Craft. London: Methuen, pp. 126–42, passim.
        Has scattered references to Auden throughout. Reprints
     1964.B2; American edition: 1972.B4.

3   DAVISON, TREVOR. "The Method of Auden's 'The Orators.'"
     Durham University Journal, n.s. 32 (June), 167–78.
        Discusses each part of "The Orators" and tries to show
     the relationship of each to the whole on the basis of an
     underlying thesis of the "dissociation of Art and Life."
     Examines separately each of the six Odes in Book Three.
     Interprets each kind of oratory as autonomous, and yet to-
     gether they are the sum which is the meaning of the book.

4   EDWARDS, THOMAS R. "September 1, 1939," in his Imagination
     and Power: A Study of Poetry on Public Themes. New York:
     Oxford University Press, pp. 203–10.
        Agrees with Auden that "September 1, 1939" is a bad
     poem; for Auden in the poem lacks "terms that can firmly
     link personal concerns and public issues." Compares the
     poem with Eliot's "Coriolan" and Yeats' "Easter 1916."

5   KALLSEN, T.J. "W.H. Auden's Supersonnet." Genre, 4 (Decem-
     ber), 329–34.
        Discusses various experimentations with the sonnet form
     and argues that Auden found the upper limits of the sonnet
     in "The Crossroads" and "The Council."

6   KING, SISTER M. JUDINE, I.H.M. "An Explication of 'At the
     Grave of Henry James' by W.H. Auden." Horizontes, 25,
     61–65.
        Auden's poem is a traditional elegy if it is defined
     "as a love-poem and a lament in which nature is pictured
     as mourning the death of the beloved shepherd." Traces
     the poem's traditional characteristics and a number of the
     images and themes characteristic of Auden. The poem
     studies "the sharply self-conscious process of the poet as
     creator-commentator" and "the dichotomy between life and
     art...."

7   KIRBY, DAVID K. "Snyder, Auden, and the New Morality." Notes
     on Contemporary Literature, 1 (January), 9–10.
        Diverse viewpoints like Auden's and Snyder's concur in
     the belief that sex is "the only genuine experience left to
     the 'average man'" and "its frank treatment in literature
     is an inevitable occurrence rather than a studied or calcu-
     lated one."

8   McDIARMID, LUCY S. "Auden and the Redeemed City: Three Allu-
     sions." Criticism, 13 (Fall), 340-50.
        Points out a number of allusions and references in
     Auden's Horae Canonicae and explores their usefulness in
     interpretation.

9   MORSE, DONALD E. "Auden's Concept and Practice of Christian
     Comedy." Michigan Academician, 4 (Summer), 29-35.
        By combining biblical elements with contemporary ele-
     ments in "For the Time Being," Auden is able to avoid both
     platitudes and cliches and yet present man's failings and
     foolish pretenses.

10   NOVAK, ROBERT. "In Brueghel's Icarus, for Instance." Wind-
     less Orchard, 6 (Summer), 48-53.
        Comments on readings and misreadings of Auden's "Musee
     des Beaux Arts"; sees the poem as existential, calling the
     human condition "absurd and alone."

11   WALSH, WILLIAM. "The Untransfigured Scene: The Personal
     Voice in Auden's Early Poetry." Studies in the Twentieth
     Century, 8 (Fall), 1-36.
        Replies to the early negative criticism of Auden's
     works, gives a history of that criticism, and explains the
     rationale behind it. Argues that Auden never grew "facilely
     inhuman" as is charged, but rather "from his youthful
     bird's-eye view...he descends closer and closer...to the
     earth of our common life" and like Antaeus grows stronger
     from its touch. Another Time marks Auden's final descent
     to earth and "this anxious human life."

12   WEATHERHEAD, A. KINGSLEY. "British Leftist Poetry of the
     Nineteen Thirties." Michigan Quarterly Review, 10 (Winter),
     12-22.
        Though not himself engaged actively in leftist politics,
     Auden's verse techniques and attitudes served as models for
     others. Supplies background of the English leftist move-
     ment and compares it to American leftist attitudes among
     writers.

1972 A BOOKS

1   BEALL, EUGENIE REAGAN. "'By Amor Rationalis Led': The
     Dantesque Element in the Poetry of W.H. Auden." Ph.D.
     dissertation, Wayne State University.
        Auden shares with Dante the "effort to express poetic-
     ally the nature and operation of Amor Rationalis, human

1972

love." This affinity with Dante appears throughout Auden's work. Abstracted in <u>Dissertation Abstracts International</u>, 33 (May 1973), 6338-A.

2 BLOOMFIELD, B.C. AND EDWARD MENDELSON. <u>W.H. Auden, A Biblio-graphy, 1924-1969</u>. Second edition. Charlottesville, Virginia: University Press of Virginia, 420 pp.
    Revised and expanded edition of Bloomfield's first edition of this bibliography which listed Auden's works through 1955. A descriptive bibliography like the first edition it provides lists of reviews, notes on the composition, descriptions of bindings, and adds a note on dust jackets. The section on bibliography and criticism contains 577 items and a list of dissertations and theses. Considered by most critics to be the definitive bibliography.

3 DOWLING, DEAN EDWARD. "A Concordance to the Poetry of W.H. Auden." Ph.D. dissertation, Columbia University.
    Indexes the primary words in <u>About the House, Academic Graffiti, City Without Walls, Collected Longer Poems, Collected Shorter Poems, Epistle to a Godson, and Homage to Clio.</u> Abstracted in <u>Dissertation Abstracts International</u>, 33 (May 1973), 6352-A.

4 DUCHENE, FRANCOIS. <u>The Case of the Helmeted Airman; a Study of W.H. Auden's Poetry</u>. London: Chatto & Windus, 228 pp.
    Auden attempts to reconcile intellect and feeling by evolving a perspective impersonal and detached like that of "the hawk or the helmeted airman." He thus "does not so much affirm feelings as seek the setting for his inner world." Duchene sees this as the essential difference between Auden and Yeats or Eliot with whom he is frequently compared. To illustrate his assertions about Auden Duchene touches on many poems and essays but only indirectly analyzes the poems as poems.

5 FREEMAN, FRANCES A. "Functional Ambiguity in Early Poems by W.H. Auden." Ph.D. dissertation, Northwestern University.
    Auden allows the speakers in his poems "to play with words and ideas...to reveal their ambivalent feelings." Abstracted in <u>Dissertation Abstracts International</u>, 33 (April 1973), 5721-A.

6 MOAN, MARGARET A. "Auden and His Audience: A Stylistic Study of W.H. Auden's Poetry in the Nineteen Thirties." Ph.D dissertation, Temple University.

106

Auden's desire to communicate with a broader audience explains the greater syntactical clarity of his later volumes in the thirties. Examines Auden's "syntactic choices" in the poems of the thirties. Abstracted in Dissertation Abstracts International, 32 (June 1972), 6991-A.

1972 B SHORTER WRITINGS

1 ANDRE, MICHAEL. "A Talk with W.H. Auden." Unmuzzled Ox, 1 (Summer), 5-11.
    An account, from memory, of a question and answer session with Auden, March 1, 1972. Auden speaks of influences, poets he likes and dislikes, and his own work. He explains the meaning of "June Bride" in the Orators. Included in 1974.B1.

2 BAYLEY, JOHN. "The Greatness of Auden." Books and Bookmen, 18 (October), 9-11.
    Auden brought out into the open a private world and thereby created a climate wherein poets like Lowell and Berryman could write successful "confessional" poems. They are "stepsons" to Auden and have "learnt the lesson he had to teach." Also reviews Duchene's The Case of the Helmeted Airman.

3 BONE, CHRISTOPHER. "W.H. Auden in the 1930's: The Problem of Individual Commitment to Political Action." Albion, 4, no. 1, 3-11.
    Offers a close reading of "Spain" to illustrate Auden's belief in "the moral necessity of immediate action." At the same time the poem bears the stamp of "clinical detachment." The problems of individual commitment, the meaning of freedom, and the necessity of political action are dominant concerns also in Journey to a War. Out of it eventually is to come Auden's denial of "the possibility of any meaningful action on earth."

4 BROOKS, CLEANTH. A Shaping Joy: Studies in the Writer's Craft. New York: Harcourt, Brace, Jovanovich, pp. 126-42.
    American edition of 1971.B2.

5 DAALDER, JOOST. "W.H. Auden's 'Another Time.'" Concerning Poetry, 5 (Spring), 65-66.
    Interprets "Another Time" as an argument for appreciating the present, for making the "conscious, religious" choice of "I Am."

1972

6 DAVIE, DONALD. "The Hawk's Eye," in his <u>Thomas Hardy and British Poetry</u>. New York: Oxford University Press, pp. 105-29, passim.
      Auden values in Hardy "his way of looking at life from a very great height." Studies this aspect of Auden. <u>See</u> especially pp. 116-28.

7 HALPERN, DANIEL. "Interview with W.H. Auden." <u>Antaeus</u>, 5: 134-149.
      Auden talks about his life, writers and others who have influenced him, and his interests.

8 JOHNSON, RICHARD A. "Auden and the Art of Clarification." <u>Yale Review</u>, 61 (Summer), 496-516.
      Auden's poems help us to see better because they are "instruments of vision," and the particular perspective they supply is Auden's "highly developed comic sense." The end is knowledge. Uses this thesis to interpret "Consider" and "On This Island."

9 _____. "Auden's Architecture of Humanism." <u>Virginia Quarterly Review</u>, 48 (Winter), 95-116.
      A close reading of the sequence of poems "Thanksgiving for a Habitat." These poems "celebrate...the fullness and variety of man's position as a complex, limited, temporal being." Focuses on man as fabricator--of houses and of poems.

10 KENNEDY, R.C. "The Classical Stance: W.H. Auden's Poetry." <u>Art International</u>, 16 (20 January), 60-65, 71
      Auden's interest in order, objectivity, form reason, and style, all reflected by this achievement in verse and prose, means he is anti-romantic and classical. Explores the meaning of these terms and applies them to Auden's shorter poems.

11 QUEENER, LEA G. "Contiguity Figures: An Index to the Language-World Relationships in Auden's Poetry." in <u>Studies in Interpretation</u>. Edited by Esther M. Doyle and Virginia H. Floyd. Amsterdam: Rodopi N.V., pp. 37-98.
      A close reading of Auden's "The Questioner Who Sits So Sly" to study his uses of figures based on contiguous relationships (synechdoche, metonymy, etc.). He seems to prefer them to those based on comparison alone. Argues that these choices reflect Auden's view of reality.

12 TURPIN, ELIZABETH R. "Rhetoric and Rhythm in Twentieth-Century Sonnets by Hopkins, Auden, Frost, Cummings, Thomas, and Merrill Moore." Ph.D. dissertation, Texas A&M University.

Examines point of view and technique in selections from
Auden's traditional and experimental sonnets. Abstracted
in Dissertation Abstracts International, 33 (February 1973),
4368-A.

1973 A   BOOKS

1   BUELL, FREDERICK. W.H. Auden as a Social Poet. Ithaca, New
    York: Cornell University Press, 196 pp.
        The social aspect of Auden's verse will make him last
    as a major poet. Three chapters set the stage of political
    and literary "ferment" in which Auden began his career and
    discuss the relationship of a writer to his political
    society. The remaining chapters trace the development of
    Auden's search for a coherent "cultural-political" identity.

2   JOHNSON, RICHARD A. Man's Place: An Essay on Auden. Ithaca,
    New York: Cornell University Press, 252 pp.
        Title refers to Auden's "opposing those forces that have
    reduced our sense of our place in the world." Auden is
    treated as a philosophical poet in the sense that poetry to
    him is "not simply...a means of saying but...a primary mode
    of discovering and knowing." Poems, then, are "paradigms
    of existence" and are Auden's attempts at defining what it
    is to be human. Examines the poems after 1940 largely from
    an ontological point of view.

3   LONG, CHARLES H. "The Quest Dialectic: The Jungian and
    Kierkegaardian Quest for Unity in W.H. Auden's 'The Quest,'
    New Year Letter, and For the Time Being." Ed.D. disser-
    tation, Ball State University.
        Explicates the sonnets and the two long poems from a
    perspective combining Jung and Kierkegaard, upon which, it
    is argued, Auden constructed his own metaphysic. Ab-
    stracted in Dissertation Abstracts International, 34
    (February 1974), 5187-A.

1973 B   SHORTER WRITINGS

1   CROSSMAN, RICHARD. "Remembering and Forgetting--W.H. Auden
    Talks to Richard Crossman about Poetry." The Listener, 89
    (22 February), 238-40.
        Crossman and Auden reminisce about their days at Oxford
    and their political opinions held then, and discuss their
    present attitudes towards their pasts.

1973

2   DAALDER, JOOST. "Yeats and Auden: Some Verbal Parallels."
       Notes & Queries, 20 (September), 334-35.
          Finds "definite" echoes of Yeats in Auden's "1929,"
       "Lullaby," and "In Memory of W.B. Yeats."

3   ELLMANN, RICHARD, AND ROBERT O'CLAIR. "W.H. Auden," in their
       The Norton Anthology of Modern Poetry. New York: W.W.
       Norton, pp. 734-36.
          A brief general introduction for college students,
       setting Auden in relation to his contemporaries and his
       own statements about the uses and values of art. Follow-
       ing the preface are annotated selections of Auden's poems
       from 1928-1951.

4   FLEISSNER, ROBERT F. "How Far Do We Go? Auden's 'Moon
       Landing.'" Contemporary Poetry, 1 (Winter), 37-41.
          In "Moon Landing" Auden argues for more energy to be
       expended on "conquering the 'inner space' of the mind"
       and indicts "modern man collectively." Points out pas-
       sages in the poem that seem insulting, sneering, and false.

5   FULLER, JOHN. "W.H. Auden's First Published Poems." Notes
       & Queries, 20 (September), 333-34.
          Identifies and reprints two of Auden's contributions
       to The Gresham, Auden's school magazine, "Dawn," in 10
       (16 December 1922), 23; and "Nightfall," in 10 (9 June
       1923), 65.

6   _____. "W.H. Auden, 1907 to 1973." The Listener, 90
       (4 October), 439.
          Reminiscence of "unenthralling" meetings with Auden
       over the years, but of being under his "spell" through the
       poems.

7   HYDE, VIRGINIA M. "The Pastoral Formula of W.H. Auden and
       Piero di Cosimo." Contemporary Literature, 14 (Summer),
       332-46.
          Auden finds a model of "anti-idyllic realism" in the
       art of Piero di Cosimo. Outlines the traditions and con-
       ventions of the pastoral forms and examines Auden's use of
       them and the source of his view in Cosimo's "hard primitiv-
       ism."

8   HOPE, FRANCIS. "Meeting Point." New Statesman, 86 (2 Novem-
       ber), 645-46.
          Personal anecdote of Auden at a dinner party where, Hope
       confesses, he tried to impress Auden, who "seemed to talk
       entirely in the English bourgeous idiom...."

9   JAMES, CLIVE. "Auden's Achievement." Commentary, 56 (De-
      cember), 53-58.
          Reviews Auden's long career; argues that knowing about
      Auden's homosexuality "does nothing to diminish his poetry
      --quite the opposite." Comments on the effect of Auden's
      sexual nature on his ideas and attitudes expressed in the
      poems.

10   JURAK, MIRKO. "Dramaturgic Concepts in the English Group
      Theatre: The Totality of Artistic Involvement." Modern
      Drama, 16 (June), 81-86.
          Recounts the dramaturgic views of the Group Theatre
      (primarily as expressed in Auden's "Manifesto"), the re-
      actions of critics to these views, and the historical sig-
      nificance such views have acquired.

11   KERMODE, FRANK AND JOHN HOLLANDER. "W.H. Auden," in Modern
      British Literature. New York: Oxford University Press,
      pp. 583-86.
          A general introduction to Auden, emphasizing the back-
      ground both literary and political that produced his
      special point of view. Includes a brief biography and
      commentary on his career and then selections of poems from
      1938-1966, with annotations. May be found in Oxford An-
      thology of English Literature, Vol. II, New York: Oxford
      University Press, pp. 2091-94.

12   LePAGE, P.V. "Some Reasons for Rhyme in 'Musee des Beaux
      Arts.'" The Yearbook of English Studies, 3: 253-58.
          Discusses structure, tone, and rhymes of "Musee des
      Beaux Arts" as Auden's deliberate choices to "force the
      prosaic and poetic actions into coalescence."

13   LIEBERMAN, LAWRENCE. "Survivor: A Last Oak Leaf, the Critic
      in the Poet." Yale Review, 62 (Winter), 269-77.
          Reviews Epistle to a Godson and Other Poems wherein
      Auden advocates that the young become "a hardy crop of
      rugged caretakers of our future." Like Yeats, he advises
      attention to craft, carrying "it off with the insouciance
      of a casual man shooting the breeze, but secretly ruminat-
      ing in strictest prosody." See pp. 274-77.

14   MILLARD, GEOFFREY. "Auden's Common Prayer: 'In Praise of
      Limestone.'" English (London), 22 (Autumn), 105-109.
          Relates types of persons to types of rock and land-
      scape. The "best and the worst" have left the limestone
      landscape. The stoics like granite; the creative like
      soft clays, "immoderate soils." Limestone has a primitive

1973

> tribal warmth. "One belongs to, one is intimately ac-
> quainted with the secrets of, and one shares in, the
> 'Common Prayer,' in spite of its over-all lack of purpose."
> It is a prayer for a return to the womb.

15   NOVAK, ROBERT. "Auden's Advice to the Young." Windless
     Orchard, 13 (Spring), 34-37.
        Compares the advice given to Spender's son in "Epistle
     to a Godson" to advice Auden, now sixty-five, has given
     over the years. Except that now his words have a Christian
     slant, he is still saying "rejoice. Be glad."

*16 PALIWAL, B.B. "W.H. Auden's The Shield of Achilles." Punjab
     University Research Bulletin, 4 (April), 211-15.
        Not seen. Cited in Abstracts of English Studies, 17, 9,
     p. 591.

17   RICKS, CHRISTOPHER. "Natural Linguistics." Parnassus:
     Poetry in Review, 1 (Spring-Summer), 27-37.
        Review of Epistle to a Godson and Other Poems with
     special attention to Auden's "Talking to--" poems. Em-
     phasizes Auden's delight in language and names.

18   SMITH, JANET ADAM. "Auden and the 'Listener.'" The Listener,
     90 (18 October), 532-34.
        An account of the difficulties in the thirties of con-
     vincing the editors to print Auden's poems. Lists the
     poems published then and comments briefly on them.

19   SPENDER, STEPHEN. "W.H. Auden (1907-1973)." Partisan Review,
     40, no. 3, 546-48.
        An assessment of Auden, written the week after his
     death, by one who had known him from youth. Attempts to
     point out Auden's originality and some of his feelings in
     the last years. Reprinted: 1973.B20.

20   _____, et. al. "W.H. Auden (1907-1973)." New Statesman,
     86 (5 October), 478-80.
        Personal tributes by Spender, Larkin, Monteith, Bet-
     jeman, Kermode, Coldstream, published the day after Auden's
     funeral. Spender's is reprinted 1973.B19; Coldstream's
     under the title of "A Portrait" 1975.A6.

1974 A   BOOKS

1   GREEN, TIMOTHY E. "The Comic Art of W.H. Auden: Theory and
     Practice." Ph.D. dissertation, Texas Technological
     University.

Relates Auden's comic view of humanity to his religious
view. A Christian-comic view laughs with, not at the weaknesses of man, "forgiveness being an essential component of
genuine laughter." Abstracted in Dissertation Abstracts
International, 35 (April 1975), 6712-A.

2   JOHNSON, SUSAN W. "The Poetry of W.H. Auden: A Way of
       Praising." Ph.D. dissertation, University of Virginia.
          Auden's career is unified by his concern for man.
       Images recur throughout but his perspective expands and
       deepens; his expressed goals in the later poetry testify
       to his development: he "begins with a sense of threat
       and ends with praise...." Abstracted in Dissertation Ab-
       stracts International, 35 (October 1974), 2272-73-A.

1974 B   SHORTER WRITINGS

1   ANDRE, KENNETH M. "Levertov, Creeley, Wright, Auden, Gins-
       berg, Corso, Dickey: Essays and Interviews with Contem-
       porary American Poets." Ph.D. dissertation, Columbia
       University.
          The emphasis is on the other poets listed, not Auden.
       For the interview with Auden see 1972.B1. Abstracted in
       Dissertation Abstracts International, 36 (December 1975),
       3681-82-A.

2   CALLAN, EDWARD. "Auden Triumphant." Journal of Modern
       Literature, 3 (April), 1055-62.
          Reviews City without Walls and Epistle to a Godson and
       comments on New Year Greeting, a privately printed pamph-
       let.
          Auden "seeks to pitch three tents: one for Horace, one
       for Goethe, and one for Isaiah." The theme of both col-
       lections is restoration. Auden restores by calling in
       "the Horatian virtues to redress Romantic excess," includ-
       ing the present day excesses. Concludes with high praise
       for Bloomfield's and Mendelson's bibliography and with an
       appraisal of Duchene's The Case of the Helmeted Airman.

3   _____. "Exorcising Mittenhofer." London Magazine, 14
       (April-May), 73-85.
          An expansion of the ideas in 1974.B2. Here Dag Hammar-
       skjold replaces Goethe as the middle figure of the trium-
       virate representing imagination, reason and belief. Mit-
       tenhofer is a caricature of the Romantic, divinely inspired
       artist, who in Elegy for Young Lovers "contrives to sacri-
       fice actual lives on the altar of art." Explores Auden's
       last poems as the conclusion of a lifetime of exorcising
       Mittenhofer.

1974

4   COHEN, EDWARD H. "Auden's 'A Shock.'" <u>Notes on Contemporary
    Literature</u>, 4, no. 4, 7-8.
        Interprets "A Shock" as self-discovery; the "I" of the
    poem discovers a self unprepared for the "harsh realities
    of the twentieth century" when he is "frisked by a cop for
    weapons."

5   DAALDER, JOOST. "W.H. Auden's 'The Shield of Achilles' and
    Its Sources." <u>Journal of the Australasian Universities
    Language and Literature Association</u>, 42: 186-98.
        Because Auden knew Greek, critics mistakenly think he
    worked directly from Homer in writing "The Shield of
    Achilles." Daalder shows instead the relationship between
    Auden's poem and his real sources: John Chapman's
    <u>Achilles' Shield</u>, A.T. Murray's <u>Homer</u>, John Keats' <u>Ode on
    a Grecian Urn</u>, and John Milton's <u>Paradise Lost</u>.

6   DEEDY, JOHN. "Managing Literary History." <u>Commonweal</u>, 101
    (October 11), 38-41.
        Discusses the pros and cons of acceding to Auden's re-
    quest that all his correspondence be destroyed; illustrates
    various reactions by quoting Auden's friends and acquaint-
    ances who possess his letters.

7   FISHER, A.S.T. "Auden's Juvenilia." <u>Notes & Queries</u>, n.s.
    21 (October), 370-73.
        Describes Auden's poems written before May 1926. They
    show influences of Hardy, Housman, and Edward Thomas.

8   GOWDA, H.H. ANNIAH. "W.H. Auden: A Tribute." <u>Literary Half
    Yearly</u>, 15, no. 1, 16-21.
        Transcript of a commemorative talk on Auden, praising
    both his contributions to modern verse and to poetic
    drama. Praises especially the "eclectic" quality in his
    work.

9   GRANT, DAMIAN. "Verbal Events." <u>Critical Quarterly</u>, 16
    (Spring), 81-86.
        Reviews <u>Epistle to a Godson and Other Poems</u>. Considers
    Auden to be working at "a wholesale scaling-down of human
    self-importance," an essentially anti-romantic position.

10 JOHNSON, WENDELL STACY. "Auden, Hopkins, and the Poetry of
    Reticence." <u>Twentieth Century Literature</u>, 20 (July),
    165-71.
        Shows parallels between Hopkins and Auden, who con-
    sidered Hopkins a major poet. Auden employs Hopkins'

voice in "Petition" and some of his matter in later poems.
Auden valued reticence and disliked what he thought in
Hopkins was a lack of reticence about personal feelings.

11   LAW, PAM. "A Ritual of Homage for W.H. Auden." Poetry Aus-
     tralia, 10 (first quarter), 83–88.
          A summing-up prose elegy of Auden and his work. Com-
     ments on Auden's technique and responds to adverse criti-
     cisms of it; explains Auden's apparent frivolity and
     pedanticism as his "rococo manner"; and testifies to a
     consistency in Auden's work by a series of Auden-has-always
     statement: "Auden has always disliked the mass.... He
     has always been critical of our civilisation...."; and
     others implying the always. Concludes with regret for our
     loss "of a voice whose joyful irreverence we can ill af-
     ford to lose...."

12   MILLARD, G.C. "Poetry Nonetheless: Early Auden." Comtempor-
     ary Review (London), 225 (November), 268–72.
          Numerous early poems demonstrate Auden's concern with
     the poet's craft rather than with propaganda, charges to
     the contrary notwithstanding. Analyzes "Consider This and
     in Our Time."

13   NEWMAN, MICHAEL. "The Art of Poetry." Paris Review, 14
     (Spring), 32–69.
          In New York Auden answers the interviewer about his per-
     sonal preferences and opinions on people, politics, reli-
     gion, and art.

14   OTTO, LON JULES. "Medieval Prosody and Four Modern Poets:
     The Accentual Poetry of Hopkins, Hardy, Pound, and Auden"
     Ph.D. dissertation, Indiana University.
          Auden, in contrast to the other three poets, uses ac-
     centual rhythms "as a mask, to universalize heroic actions
     and elegiac themes, or to underline modern distortions of
     those actions and themes." Abstracted in Dissertation
     Abstracts International, 35 (January 1975), 4447-48-A.

15   PESCHMANN, HERMANN. "W.H. Auden: 1907-1973." English, 23
     (Spring), 3-4.
          Brief biographical comments, personal reminiscences,
     and survey of Auden's principal books of poems. Critical
     debate must decide whether the later poems are better than
     the early. "What is urgently needed is a variorum edition,
     or at least a new Collected Poems, in chronological order,
     reprinting all the poems in the wording of their first
     appearance in book form."

16 REES, SAMUEL. "'What Instruments We Have': An Appreciation
    of W.H. Auden." Anglo-Welsh Review, 24 (Summer), 9-18.
        Surveys Auden's career by means of the elegies he had
    written, beginning with that on Yeats. "Instruments" is a
    metaphor for what we should praise in Auden: "For the
    precision psycho-explorative and psycho-surgical instru-
    ments he employed with such care, for the sensitive re-
    cording instruments by which he measured the health and
    weather of western culture, and for the musical instruments
    that he orchestrated into the collected poetry of over
    forty years."

17 SARANG, VILAS. "Articles in the Poetry of W.H. Auden."
    Language and Style, 7: 77-90.
        Reviewing the statistical data and examining the char-
    acteristics of Auden's verse show that Auden was fully
    conscious of the effects produced by using or not using
    the definite and indefinite articles. Compares late poems
    to early.

18 SPEARS, MONROE K. "In Memoriam W.H. Auden." Sewanee Review,
    82 (Fall), 672-81.
        Praises Auden as a "wise and good man" entirely without
    "self-importance and pretentiousness," one who sees com-
    munity as "basic to all religious faith." Describes
    Auden's attitudes and ideals in his last years, illustrat-
    ing briefly from Nones and About the House.

19 THURLEY, GEOFFREY. "W.H. Auden: The Image as Instance," in
    The Ironic Harvest. New York: St. Martin's Press, pp.
    54-78.
        For Auden, writing is the pursuit of self-knowledge,
    which pursuit inevitably backfires by producing "a refined
    sense of personal guilt." Auden's poetry supplies "further
    evidence of the self-alienation of the intellectual in the
    twentieth century." Auden's contribution to a poetic
    method for modern poets is the montage of social observa-
    tions. Discusses Audan's images as general and abstract,
    both a strength and a weakness.

20 THWAITE, ANTHONY. "W.H. Auden: 1907-1973." Literary Half
    Yearly, 15, no. 1, 1-11.
        Responds to some of the negative criticisms of Auden
    like charges of arrested adolescence, obscurity, and po-
    litical dogmatism. Answers at length the accusation that
    his work declined after 1939, pointing to single poems
    from The Shield of Achilles through Epistle to a Godson
    "which can properly stand alongside his best earlier work."

21 WOODCOCK, GEORGE. "Auden--Critic and Criticized." Sewanee
    Review, 82 (Fall), 685-97.
        An aloof man who desired no official biography, Auden
    has nonetheless given autobiographical hints of the sort
    relevant to his work. Forewords and Afterwords is such a
    book. Also reviews W.H. Auden: A Bibliography (1972.A2),
    W.H. Auden as a Social Poet (1973.A1), and Man's Place:
    An Essay on Auden (1973.A2). These concentrate on works
    rather than on the man.

1975 A BOOKS

1. BARDEN, THOMAS E. "W.H. Auden: The Poet's Uses of Drama."
    Ph.D. dissertation, University of Virginia.
        A chronological study of Auden's use of the dramatic in
    all his verse, not just the plays. Finds the dramatic
    mode "central and almost instinctual" to Auden. Ab-
    stracted in Dissertation Abstracts International, 36
    (January 1976), 4473-A.

2. OLDHAM, PERRY D., JR. "The Conversational Poetry of W.H.
    Auden." Ph.D. dissertation, The University of Oklahoma.
        Auden is in the "tradition of genial discourse" and
    heir to Pope and Byron. Attempts to define the "discursive
    tradition" to which Auden belongs and distinguish it from
    other types of colloquial traditions. Abstracted in
    Dissertation Abstracts International, 35 (July 1975),
    325-A.

3. PARSONS, GERALD M. "W.H. Auden: Aspects of His Poetry and
    Criticism." Ph.D. dissertation, The University of
    Nebraska-Lincoln.
        Auden's life "can be read teleologically"; relates
    Auden's beliefs about art to his Christianity and social
    concerns. Abstracted in Dissertation Abstracts Inter-
    national, 36 (February 1976), 5324-25-A.

4   RIGGS, ERICA HELEN. "Ariel and Prospero in the Poetry and
    Criticism of W.H. Auden through 'The Sea and the Mirror.'"
    Ph.D. dissertation, University of Toronto.
        Examines closely Auden's philosophical standpoint in
    key early works and compares it with his later Christian
    outlook in "The Sea and the Mirror."

5   SEYMOUR, BETTY JEAN. "The Dyer's Hand: Kierkegaardian
    Perspectives on Person, Word, and Art Re-discovered in
    W.H. Auden." Ph.D. dissertation, Duke University.

Kierkegaard's concept of subjectivity is the crucial
influence on Auden. Relates this thesis to Auden's theories of art and language and his concept of the self.
Abstracted in Dissertation Abstracts International, 36
(January 1976), 4583-A.

6   SPENDER, STEPHEN, ed. W.H. Auden: A Tribute. New York:
MacMillan, 255 pp.
Covers practically the whole of Auden's life. Two gaps
are his first visit to Europe and his visit to Spain
during the Spanish Civil War. Spender solicited most of
the essays especially for this book. Included also are
photographs from every period and reproductions of some
manuscripts and title pages.

1975 B   SHORTER WRITINGS

1   ATLAS, JAMES. "Earth, Receive an Honored Guest." Poetry,
126 (June), 175-79.
Review of Thank You, Fog: Last Poems. Uses the occasion to review Auden's lifework, commenting favorably on
his last book as seen from that perspective. Auden has
been "the prime protector of our language...when the pro-
tection of its virtues required particular vigilance."
Replies to most of the negative criticisms by well-known
critics over the years (like Jarrell, Wilson and Ellmann)
and concludes by observing, "The pleasure in reading him
is in always being sure to find, for all occasions, words
better than one's own."

2   BATESON, F.W. "Auden's Last Poems." Essays in Criticism, 25
(July), 383-90.
Reviews Auden's Thank You, Fog. Uses the theme of
Auden's "Silliness" to comment on Auden's various books,
such as on Auden's silliness in revising the definite
article out of many of his poems reprinted in Collected
Shorter Poems, 1927-1957. Includes descriptions of Bateson's meetings with Auden and Bateson's observation, "I
have found my admiration for Auden has waned.... I have
found nothing in Thank You, Fog to revive my earlier en-
thusiasm." Analyzes "A Thanksgiving."

3   BERGONZI, BERNARD. "Auden and the Audenesque." Encounter,
44 (February), 65-75.
Lists and describes the Audenesque, the style of Auden
"that became a collective idiom." Traces from the early
poems Auden's use of definite articles, adjectives, sur-
prising similes, personified abstractions, and possessives.

Finds most impressive Auden's poems with "a geographical or topographical structure."

4 CONOLLY, CYRIL. "Remembering Auden." Encounter, 44 (March), 90-93.
   Reminiscence of Auden from a meeting in Valencia, May 1937, until a final meeting in January 1973. Quotes from personal letters, which, Connolly says, he disobeyed Auden by keeping. Reprinted 1975.A6.

5 LYNEN, JOHN F. "Forms of Time in Modern Poetry." Queen's Quarterly, 82 (Autumn), 344-64.
   Explores the analogy of modern times with the ancient, of contemporary scenes with primitive, and of brief actions with longer processes, as Auden elaborates them in "The Shield of Achilles," and other poems. See especially pp. 350-52.

6 McDIARMID, LUCY S. AND JOHN McDIARMID. "Artifice and Self-Consciousness in Auden's The Sea and the Mirror." Contemporary Literature, 16 (Summer), 353-77.
   A close reading of the personae of The Sea and the Mirror in respect to their styles of speech. They speak self-consciously, recognizing their artificiality and "unreality." Reversing the positions in The Tempest, Auden makes Prospero "the most naive and the least self-conscious" and Caliban "the most sophisticated."

7 MEGAW, MOIRA. "Auden's First Poems." Essays in Criticism, 25 (July), 378-82.
   Reviews the facsimile edition of Auden's Poems 1928, reproduced for the Ilkley Literature Festival, April 24, 1973. Considers most of the poems vague and false, thinks Auden at his best in two landscape poems ("The Watershed" and "The Letter"), and considers the book "no major contribution to his poems in print."

8 PADEN, FRANCES FREEMAN. "Riddling in W.H. Auden's 'The Wanderer.'" Speech Monographs, 42 (March), 42-46.
   Auden's riddling techniqe in "The Wanderer" illustrates his use of the riddle as a device in which his personae who "find themselves in a threatening world" may, like the ancients, place "great trust...to cure their ills and bring them good fortune in times of crisis." Offers a close reading of the poem from the standpoint of one preparing an oral interpretation of the poem.

1975

9 SMITH, ELTON EDWARD. "Wystan Hugh Auden: The Tyranny of
   Mind," in his The Angry Young Men of The Thirties. Cross-
   currents/Modern Critiques. Carbondale, Illinois: Southern Illinois University Press, pp. 93-133.
      Auden dominated, fascinated, and influenced the "ideas
   if not the styles" of his friends. Discusses Auden's development as recorded by Spender in World Within World
   (1951). Uses Spender as a foil by examining his assertions
   for accuracies and inaccuracies about Auden.

10 STELOFF, FRANCES. "W.H. Auden." Journal of Modern Literature, 4 (April), 877-79.
      Steloff recounts her first meeting with Auden and a
   few anecdotes about him in relation to the Gotham Book
   Mart: how he gave benefit readings, picked up a copy of
   Fanny Hill, and had given manuscripts to friends to help
   them financially.

11 WAIDSON, H.M. "Auden and German Literature." The Modern
   Language Review, 70 (April), 347-65.
      Attempts to "summarize some of the poet's literary
   interest as observed through the perspective of German
   associations...." Examines Auden's life and works in
   respect to this theme, compares themes in Auden to
   German counterparts, and relates materials in some of
   Auden's latest poems (About the House, City Without Walls,
   Epistle to a Godson) to their Austrian associations.

12 WILDE, ALAN. "Language and Surface: Isherwood and the
   Thirties." Contemporary Literature, 16 (Autumn), 478-91.
      About Isherwood and his relation to his narrators, but
   includes comments on Auden. Uses The Dog Beneath the Skin
   to explain Isherwood's purposes in his The Berlin Stories.

1976 A BOOKS - NONE

1976 B SHORTER WRITINGS

1 ANON. "Auden at Kirchstetten, 1973." The South Atlantic
   Quarterly, 75 (Winter), 8-19.
      Account of "a friendly chat" with Auden in Kirchstetten
   by one "who happened to pass by" on the way from visiting
   the grave of the Austrian poet Josef Weinheber. Describes
   Auden, his house and grounds, and some of his activities
   there.

Index

Able at Times to Cry (As He Is),
1965.B30
About the House, 1965.B15; 1966.
B5; 1967.B3; 1969.A9; 1970.
A1, A4
Address for a Prize Day, 1963.A2;
1970.A1
"Advance Guard," 1934.B9
Age of Anxiety, The, 1947.B5;
1949.A1, B2, B9; 1951.A1,
B10; 1959.A1; 1963.B1;
1964.A2, B6, B7; 1965.A2, B3,
B16; 1967.A1, A2; 1968.A4,
1969.A4, A9; 1970.A1, A4, A7;
1973.A2; 1974.A1, B14;
1975.A1
Ahern, Eckoe M., 1962.B1
"Airmen, Politics and Psycho-
Analysis," 1935.B7
"Allegory in Auden's The Age of
Anxiety," 1965.B3
Allen, Walter, 1952.B1
"Allotropy of the Auden Group,
The," 1963.B5
Allott, Kenneth, 1936.B1; 1937.B1;
1939.B1
"'All We Are Stares Back at What
We Are': A Note on Auden,"
1959.B7
Alonso to Ferdinand, 1969.A8
"Altered Auden, An," 1958.B6
Alvarez, A., 1958.B1
Amor Loci, 1972.B6
"Analysis of Guilt: Poetry of
W.H. Auden, The," 1965.B18
Anderson, D.M., 1959.B1

Andre, Kenneth Michael, 1972.B1;
1974.B1
Aney, Edith T., 1954.B1
"Anglo-Saxon and Middle English
Influences in the Poetry of
W.H. Auden," 1969.A1
"Angry Young Poet of the Thir-
ties," 1963.B4
"Anima Naturaliter Christiana,"
1967.B11
"Annotated Checklist of the
Works of W.H. Auden (1924-
1957), An," 1958.A1, B2
Anon., 1937.B2; 1938.B1; 1956.B1,
B2; 1957.B1; 1970.B1;
1976.B1
Another Time, 1944.B5; 1949.A1;
1951.A1; 1963.B7; 1964.A2;
1969.A5; 1970.A7; 1971.B11;
1972.A6; 1975.B9
Another Time, 1972.B5
Ansen, Alan, 1956.B3
Anthem for St. Cecilia's Day
(Song for St. Cecilia's Day),
1967.A3
Appel, Benjamin, 1940.B1
"Ariel and Prospero in the Poetry
and Criticism of W.H. Auden
Through 'The Sea and the
Mirror,'" 1975.A4
Armytage, W.H.G., 1969.B1
Arnold, Leslie E., 1968.A1
"Art as Communion: Auden's 'The
Sea and the Mirror,'"
1966.B21
"Articles in the Poetry of
W.H. Auden," 1974.B17

INDEX

INDEX

Bluestone, Max, 1961.B2
Bogan, Louise, 1970.B3
Bone, Christopher, 1972.B3
Bowen, C., 1970.B4
Boyer, Robert H., 1969.A1
Bradbury, John M., 1948.B2
Braybrooke, Neville, 1952.B2;
 1953.B1
Brenner, Rica, 1941.B1
Brewer, D.S., 1957.B3
Bride in the 30's, A, 1965.B9;
 1969.B2
"British Leftist Poetry of the
 Nineteen Thirties," 1971.B12
"British Poetry of Social Protest
 in the 1930's: The Problem
 of Belief in the Poetry of
 W.H. Auden, C. Day Lewis,
 'Hugh MacDiarmid,' Louis
 MacNeice, and Stephen
 Spender," 1954.B1
"British Poetry of the Spanish
 Civil War," 1961.B5
"Britten and Documentary,"
 1963.B15
Brooke-Rose, Christine, 1963.B1
Brooks, Benjamin Gilbert,
 1947.B1
Brooks, Cleanth, 1939.B3;
 1960.B2; 1964.B1, B2;
 1971.B2; 1972.B4
Brophy, James D., 1970.B2
Brothers, Who When the Sirens
 Roar (A Communist to Others).
 1934.B9; 1960.A1; 1969.B11;
 1970.A4
Bruehl, William J., 1966.A1;
 1967.B2
Bucolics, 1965.A4; 1973.A2, B7
Buell, Frederick H., 1970.A3;
 1973.A1
Bullough, Geoffrey, 1934.B1;
 1941.B2; 1949.B3; 1962.B4
Burgum, Edwin Berry, 1934.B2;
 1935.B1
Buried Day, The, 1960.B5
Burnham, James, 1934.B3
"'By Amor Rationalis Led': The
 Dantesque Element in the
 Poetry of W.H. Auden,"
 1972.A1

Byer, James Edwin, 1971.A1

Caliban to the Audience, 1969.A8
Callan, Edward, 1958.A1, B2, B3;
 1959.A1; 1963.B2, B3;
 1965.B3, B4; 1966.B2;
 1967.B3, B4; 1970.B5;
 1974.B2, B3
Calypso (Driver, drive faster
 and make a good run),
 1970.A4
Carruth, Hayden, 1951.B1, B2
Case of the Helmeted Airman, The:
 A Study of W.H. Auden's
 Poetry, 1972.A4
Casino, 1970.A1
Cavanaugh, William C., 1961.B3
Cave of Making, The, 1970.A3;
 1973.A2
Cave of Nakedness, The, 1968.A4;
 1973.A2
Challenge to Tom Harrison,
 1938.B4
Change of Air, A, 1964.B16;
 1965.A2
"Changes of Attitude and Rhetoric
 in Auden's Poetry,"
 1941.B5
Changes of Heart: A Study of
 the Poetry of W.H. Auden,
 1969.A4
Charney, Maurice, 1960.B3
Chase, Richard Volney, 1949.B4
Chaturvedi, B.N., 1967.B5
Chimneys Are Smoking, the Crocus
 Is Out in the Border (Two
 Worlds), 1968.A4; 1969.B2
Chittick, V.L.O., 1963.B4
Chorus (Doom is dark and deeper
 than any sea-dingle) (The
 Wanderer) (Something Is
 Bound to Happen), 1948.B1;
 1951.A1; 1972.A5; 1973.A2,
 B9; 1975.B8
"Christian Themes in English
 Poetry of the Twentieth
 Century," 1964.B14
Christmas 1940, 1970.A4
City, The (The Quest V), 1974.B2
City Without Walls, 1970.B4;
 1974.B2

125

INDEX

Clancy, Joseph, 1955.B1; 1959.B2
Clark, Vera F.W., 1969.A2
"Classical Stance, The:
  W.H. Auden's Poetry,"
  1972.B10
Close, H.M., 1937.B3
Coghill, Nevill, 1948.B3;
  1949.B5
Cohen, Edward H., 1974.B4
"Coherence of Auden's The
  Orators, The," 1968.B7
"Collaboration with Auden,"
  1949.B14
Collected Longer Poems, 1970.A5
Collected Poetry of W.H. Auden,
  The (The Collected Poems),
  1945.B3, B6, B7; 1949.B2;
  1957.A1; 1965.B1; 1969.A9
Collected Shorter Poems,
  1950.B1; 1957.A1; 1964.A2;
  1969.A9; 1970.A5
"Comic Art of W.H. Auden, The:
  Theory and Practice,"
  1974.A1
"Commentary," 1961.B7
"Committed Noncombatants, The,"
  1968.B16
Common Life, The, 1973.A2
"Communication, A," 1956.B3
Communist to Others, A (Brothers
  who when the sirens roar)
  (Comrades who when the
  sirens roar), 1934.B9;
  1960.A1; 1969.B11; 1970.A4
"Compassion of W.H. Auden, The,"
  1954.B2
Compline (Horae Canonicae 6),
  1973.A2
Composer, The, 1965.A2
"Concepts of Reality in the
  Poetic Drama of W.B. Yeats,
  W.H. Auden, and T.S. Eliot,"
  1964.B22
"Concordance to the Poetry of
  W.H. Auden, A," 1972.A3
Connolly, Cyril, 1975.B4
Connors, James J., 1967.B6
Consider, 1939.B3; 1958.B1;
  1965.A2, B9, B13; 1970.A4,
  B8, 1972.A5, B8; 1973.A1, A2;
  1974.B12

Consider If You Will How Lovers
  Stand, 1970.A4
"Contiguity Figures: An Index
  to the Language-World
  Relationships in Auden's
  Poetry," 1972.B11
"Conversational Poetry of
  W.H. Auden, The," 1975.A2
"Conversation on Cornelia St.:
  A Dialogue with W.H. Auden,"
  1949.B7
"Conversation on Tape, A,"
  1961.B8
"Conversations with Auden,"
  1968.B11
Cook, Frederick W., 1963.B5
Cook, F.W., 1958.B6; 1960.B4;
  1962.B5
"Coriolanus and the Ascent of
  F-6: Similarities in Theme
  and Supporting Detail,"
  1961.B3
Council, The (For the Last Time),
  1971.B5
Cowley, Malcom, 1941.B3; 1945.B1
Cox, R.G., 1951.B3; 1961.B4;
  1963.B7
"Craft Interview--W.H. Auden,"
  1970.B1
Craft, Robert, 1960.B22;
  1963.B15; 1966.B17; 1969.B16
"Critical Prose of W.H. Auden,
  The," 1962.A2
Crossman, Richard, 1973.B1
Crossroads, The (The Quest III),
  1971.B5
Cultural Presupposition, The
  (Culture), 1966.B1

Daalder, Joost, 1972.B5; 1973.B2;
  1974.B5
Daiches, David, 1939.B4; 1940.B2,
  B3
Dame Kind, 1963.B13; 1965.A2;
  1966.B1
Dance of Death, The, 1934.B5, B9;
  1936.B4; 1939.B11; 1940.B4;
  1944.B5; 1951.B5; 1954.B8;
  1962.B11; 1964.A2; 1966.A1;
  1967.B5; 1968.A1, A4, B5;
  1969.A2, A9, B11; 1970.A4,

INDEX

INDEX

Falck, Colin, 1966.B4
Fall of Rome, The, 1962.B17
Family Ghosts, 1939.B3
"Father Christmas Passage in
    Auden's 'Paid on Both Sides',
    The," 1969.B3
Faulkner, Peter, 1970.B7
Fiedler, Leslie, A., 1964.B3
Fisher, A. S. T., 1974.B7
Fish in the Unruffled Lakes
    (Twelve Songs, V), 1966.B1
Fitzgerald, David, 1967.B10
"Five Notes on W. H. Auden's
    Writing,' 1932.B2
"Five Tributes," 1967.B15
Fleet Visit, 1970.A4
Fleissner, Robert F., 1973.B4
Fletcher, John Gould, 1933.B1
Flint, F. Cudworth, 1938.B6
Ford, Hugh D., 1961.B5;
    1965.B6
For Friends Only, 1973.A2
Forewords and Afterwords,
    1974.B21
"Formal Experiments in Modern
    Verse Drama," 1958.B4
"Forms of Time in Modern Poetry,"
    1975.B5
Forster, E. M., 1951.B6
For the Last Time (The Council),
    1971.B5
For the Time Being, 1944.B1, B2;
    1945.B1; 1946.B3; 1947.B1,
    B5; 1949.A1, B1; 1951.A1,
    B11; 1959.A1, B4; 1961.B9;
    1963.A2, B7; 1964.A2;
    1965.A2, A4, B16; 1966.B13;
    1967.A1, A2; 1969.A2, A4,
    A5, A9; 1970.A1, A4, A7;
    1973.A1, A3; 1974.A1;
    1975.A3
For the Time Being, 1946.B7;
    1952.B10, B11; 1956.B8;
    1963.B8; 1965.B4, B29;
    1966.A2; 1967.B17, B18;
    1968.A3, A6; 1970.B17;
    1971.B9
"'For the Time Being': Man's
    Response to the Incarnation,"
    1967.B18

"'For the Time Being': W. H.
    Auden's Christmas Oratorio,"
    1952.B10
Fowler, Helen, 1965.B7
Foxall, Edgar, 1934.B6
Frankenberg, Lloyd, 1949.B6
Fraser, G. S., 1950.B3;
    1953.B2; 1956.B5; 1959.B4;
    1960.B6; 1964.B4; 1965.B8;
    1966.B5
Freeman, Frances A., 1972.A5
Fremantle, Anne, 1944.B2;
    1945.B3; 1967.B11
Friedman, S. 1966.B6
"From Freud to Paul: The Stages
    of Auden's Ideology,"
    1945.B5
"From Myth to Allegory: A Study
    of the Poetry of W. H. Auden
    with Special Reference to the
    Poet's Intention," 1968.A2
"From the Diaries of Robert
    Craft, 1948-1968," 1969.B16
Fuller, John, 1964.B5; 1970.A5;
    1973.B5
Fuller, Roy, 1970.B8; 1973.B6
"Functional Ambiguity in Early
    Poems by W. H. Auden,"
    1972.A5

Galinsky, Hans, 1964.B6
"Gang Myth in Auden's Early
    Poetry, The," 1962.B14
"Gazebos and Gashouses,"
    1967.B9
"General View of Auden's
    Poetry, A," 1965.B32
"Generation of Auden, The,"
    1964.B7
Geography of the House, The,
    1973.A2
Gerstenberger, Donna L.
    1958.B14; 1962.B8
Get There If You Can and See the
    Land You Were Once Proud to
    Own, 1970.A4; 1973.A1
Ghosh, Prabodh Chandra,
    1965.B9
Glicksberg, Charles I.,
    1937.B4; 1938.B7

129

Hyams, C. Barry, and Karl H. Reichert, 1957.B5

Hyde, Virginia M., 1973.B7

I Am My Brother, 1960.B10; 1969.B8

"Iconographic Sources of Auden's 'Musee des Beaux Arts', The," 1961.B2

"Ideas in Auden," 1946.B3

"Idiom of W. H. Auden, The," 1947.B3

"Importance of W. H. Auden, The," 1939.B13

"In Brueghel's Icarus, for Instance," 1971.B10

"Individuals of a Group: The 1930's Poetry of W. H. Auden, C. Day Lewis and Stephen Spender," 1958.B5

In Father's Footsteps (Our Hunting Fathers), 1941.B7; 1961.B4; 1965.B9; 1966.B1

"In Memoriam W. H. Auden," 1974.B18

In Memory of Sigmund Freud, 1970.A4

In Memory of W. B. Yeats, 1965.A2; 1966.B5, B14; 1967.B4; 1970.A4

In My Own Time, 1969.B8

In Praise of Limestone, 1951.B12; 1963.B13; 1965.B17; 1969.A4; 1970.A4; 1972.B6; 1973.A2, B14

In Sickness and in Health, 1949.B4; 1969.B2

Inside the Whale, 1940.B6

"Interpretation of the Times, An: A Report on the Oral Interpretation of W. H. Auden's 'Age of Anxiety,'" 1949.B9

"Interview: W. H. Auden," 1967.B19

"Interview with Christopher Isherwood," 1965.B29

"Interview with W. H. Auden," 1972.B7

In Time of War (Sonnets from China), 1939.B7; 1951.A1; 1957.B10; 1961.B6; 1965.B23; 1968.A4; 1969.A9; 1970.A4; 1971.A2; 1975.B9

"Into the World," 1940.B2

In Transit, 1973.A2

"Introduction"
Hoggart, 1961.B6
Rexroth, 1949.B10

Irwin, John T., 1970.B13

Ischia, 1963.B13; 1968.A4; 1969.A4; 1973.A2

Isherwood, Christopher, 1937.B8; 1947.B4; 1961.B8

Islands (Bucolics 5), 1973.A2

It's Farewell to the Drawing-room's Mannerly Cry (Danse Macabre) (Song for the New Year), 1939.B2; 1970.A4

It's No Use Raising a Shout, 1970.A4, B19

It Was Easter as I Walked in the Public Garden (1929), 1936.B2; 1939.B3; 1960.B20; 1961.B4; 1965.B9; 1966.B1; 1067.B1; 1968.A4; 1969.B2, B4; 1970.A4; 1972.A5; 1973.A1; 1974.A2

I Want the Theatre to Be (Manifesto), 1935.B2; 1973.B8

Iyengar, K. R. Srinivasa, 1938.B9

Izzo, Carlo, 1952.A1; 1964.B10; 1967.B13

James, Clive, 1973.B9

Jameson, Storm, 1947.B5; 1948.B6; 1950.B5

Janet, Sister M., S. C. L., 1961.B9

January 1, 1931 (Watching in three planes from a room), 1970.A4

Jarrell, Randall, 1941.B5, B6; 1945.B5; 1947.B6; 1969.B6

Jennings, Humphrey, 1935.B4

Jew Wrecked in the German Cell, The (The Diaspora), 1955.B5

INDEX

Johnny (O the valley in the summer
where I and my John),
1970.A4
Johnson, Richard A., 1965.A3;
1972.B8, B9; 1973.A2
Johnson, Susan W., 1974.A2
Johnson, Wendell Stacy,
1974.B10
Journal of an Airman (Book II,
The Orators), 1935.B7;
1936.B4; 1951.A1; 1968.A4
Journey to a War, 1951.A1;
1964.A2; 1965.B9; 1969.A9,
B5, B11; 1972.A6, B3;
1973.A1; 1974.A2; 1975.A4
Jurak, Mirko, 1968.B5;
1969.B7; 1973.B10

Kallman, Chester, 1953.B3;
1964.B11; 1967.B14
Kallsen, T. J., 1971.B5
Kavanagh, Patrick, 1951.B7
Keller, Hans, 1952.B7
Kennedy, R. C., 1972.B10
Kerman, Joseph, 1954.B3, B4;
1956.B8; 1957.B6
Kermode, Frank, 1948.B7; 1970.B14
and John Hollander,
1973.B11
Khan, B. A., 1962.B11
"Kind of Solution, A: The
Situation of Poetry Now,"
1964.B3
King, Sister M. Judine, I. H. M.,
1971.B6
Kinney, Arthur F., 1963.B11
Kirby, David K., 1971.B7
Knoll, Robert E., 1955.B5
"Knowledge of Man in the Works
of Christopher Isherwood,
The," 1960.B12
Koch, Kenneth, 1957.B7

La Driere, J. Craig, 1934.B7
Lakes (Bucolics 4), 1970.A4;
1973.A2
"Language and Surface: Isherwood
and the Thirties," 1975.B12
Larkin, Philip, 1960.B8
"Late Auden: The Satirist as
Lunatic Clergyman," 1951.B11

Later Auden, The: From "New
Year Letter" to About the
House, 1970.A1
Lauds (Horae Canonicae 7),
1957.B3; 1973.A2
Law Like Love (Law, say the
gardeners), 1957.B10;
1965.A2
Law, Pam, 1974.B11
Lay Your Sleeping Head, My Love;
1953.B5
Leavis, F. R., 1934.B8;
1936.B3; 1960.B9
Lechlitner, Ruth, 1945.B6
"Left-Wing Poetry: A Note,"
1939.B8
Lehmann, John, 1936.B4;
1939.B10; 1940.B4;
1955.B6; 1960.B10;
1969.B8
Leinhardt, R. G., 1948.B8
Leithauser, 1970.B15
LePage, P. V., 1973.B12
Lerner, Laurence, 1960.B11
Letter, The (The Love Letter),
1972.A5; 1975.B7
Letters from Iceland, 1949.A1;
1951.A1; 1964.A2, B12;
1966.B12; 1969.A9, B5;
1970.A4; 1972.A6; 1973.A1
"Letter to W. H. Auden,"
1937.B9
"Levertov, Creeley, Wright,
Auden, Ginsberg, Corso,
Dickey: Essays and Inter-
views with Contemporary
American Poets," 1974.B1
Levin, Harry, 1944.B4
Levitin, Alexis A., 1971.A2
Lewars, Kenneth, 1968.B6
"Liberal Critics and W. H.
Auden, The," 1937.B5
Lieberman, Lawrence, 1973.B13
"Life of Literature, The,"
1948.B11; 1949.B11
Lions and Shadows, 1947.B4
"Literary Criticism of W. H.
Auden Theory and Practice,
The," 1971.A1
"Logicless Grammar in Auden-
land," 1965.B23

132

Long, Charles H., 1973.A3
"Long Walk, The: The Poetry of
W. H. Auden," 1970.B12
"Looking and Thinking Back,"
1964.B11
Look, Stranger! (On This
Island), 1944.B5; 1949.A1;
1951.A1; 1952.B13; 1961.B10;
1964.A2; 1969.A9, B11;
1970.A7; 1971.B11; 1972.A6;
1973.B9; 1975.B9
Look, Stranger (On This Island)
(Seascape), 1964.B7;
1966.A4; 1968.A1, B2;
1970.A4; 1972.B8; 1973.A2
Loose, John H., 1963.A1
"Love and Politics in the Early
Poetry of W. H. Auden,"
1966.A5
Love Feast, The, 1970.A4
Love Letter, The (The Letter),
1972.A5; 1975.B6
Lowell, Robert, et. al.,
1967.B15
"Luck in Auden," 1957.B9
Lucky, This Point in Time and
Space, 1953.B2
Lynen, John F., 1975.B5

McAleer, Edward C., 1957.B8
Macao, 1965.B1
McCoard, William B., 1949.B9
McDiarmid, John, 1975.B6
McDiarmid, Lucy S., 1971.B8
and John McDiarmid,
1975.B6
McDowell, Frederick P.,
1962.B12, B13
MacFadden, George, 1955.B7
"MacNeice, Auden, and the Art
Ballad," 1970.B13
MacNeice, Louis, 1937.B9;
1938.B10; 1966.B8; 1969.B9
Maes-Jelinek, Hena, 1960.B12
Magic Flute, The, 1957.B6;
1965.B25
Magnusson, Sigurdur A.,
1964.B12
"Major Adjectives in Poetry:
from Wyatt to Auden,"
1946.B2

"Maker of Libretti, A."
1970.B24
Making of the Auden Canon, The,
1957.A1
Malverns, The (Here on the
cropped grass), 1968.A4;
1970.A4
"Managing Literary History,"
1974.B6
Mander, John, 1961.B10
Mandle, W. F., 1969.B10
Man's Place: An Essay on Auden,
1973.A2
"Man's Tragic Dilemma in Auden
and Sophocles," 1970.B10
"Man with the Hatchet, The:
Shapiro on Auden," 1970.B25
Marken, Ronald, 1964.B13
Martin, W. G. J., 1956.B9;
1959.B5
"Marxism and English Poetry,"
1937.B13
Mason, H. A., 1948.B9
Mason, Ronald, 1948.B10
Massacre of the Innocents (from
For the Time Being), 1966.B18
"Master as Joker, The,"
1969.B4
Materer, Timothy, 1970.B16
Maxwell, D. E. S., 1969.B11
May (May with its light
behaving), 1961.B6;
1967.B1; 1970.A4
Maynard, Theodore, 1935.B5
Mazzocco, Robert, 1965.B17
"Meaning of Time in Auden's For
the Time Being," 1970.B17
"Medieval Prosody and Four
Modern Poets: The Accentual
Poetry of Hopkins, Hardy,
Pound, and Auden," 1974.B14
Meditation of Simeon, The (from
For the Time Being),
1970.B18
"Meeting Point," 1973.B8
Megaw, Moira, 1975.B7
Meiosis, 1970.B15; 1973.A2
Me, March, You Do With Your
Movements Master and Rock,
1969.B11
"Member of the Group," 1970.B21

INDEX

Poems 1928, 1966.A5; 1972.A6,
    1975.B7
"Poems of Auden and Prose
    Diathesis," 1949.B2
Poesie di W. H. Auden, 1952.A1
"Poet at Home, The," 1965.B17
Poetic Art of W. H. Auden, The,
    1965.A2
"Poetic Dramas of W. H. Auden
    and Christopher Isherwood,
    The," 1938.B13
"Poet in Praise of Limestone,
    The," 1970.B14
"Poet of Courage," 1933.B1
"Poet of Perspectives: The Style
    of W. H. Auden," 1966.A4
"Poetry and Marxism: Three
    English Poets Take Their
    Stand," 1937.B4
"Poetry and Politics: The Verse
    Drama of Auden and
    Isherwood," 1962.B8
"Poetry and Social Revolution,"
    1938.B7
Poetry Appreciation, 1968.B2
"Poetry Corner," 1936.B2
"Poetry in the 1930's: II.
    W. H. Auden and Stephen
    Spender," 1940.B3
"Poetry Nonetheless: Early
    Auden," 1974.B12
"Poetry of Auden, The,"
    1959.B6
Poetry of W. H. Auden, The,
    1965.A1
"Poetry of W. H. Auden, The"
    Brooks, B., 1947.B1
    Cox, 1961.B4
    Izzo, 1964.B10
"Poetry of W. H. Auden, The: A
    Way of Praising," 1974.A2
"Poetry of W. H. Auden,
    1941-1955, The," 1960.A1
Poetry of W. H. Auden, The: The
    Disenchanted Island, 1963.A2;
    1968.A5
"Poetry's Auden," 1970.B2
"Poetry Without Despair,"
    1966.B3

"Poets and Politics: A Study of
    the Careers of C. Day Lewis,
    Stephen Spender and W. H.
    Auden in the 1930's,"
    1967.B6
"Poet's Perspective, The,"
    1944.B6
Poggioli, Renato, 1963.B13
"Political Voice of W. H. Auden,
    The," 1970.A3
"Politics of W. H. Auden, The,"
    1934.B6
"Politics in the Early Poetry of
    W. H. Auden, 1930-1945,"
    1957.A3
"Polus Naufrangia: A Key Symbol
    in The Ascent of F6,"
    1967.B2
Porter, Peter, 1966.B12
Porteus, Hugh Gordon, 1933.B2
"Postscript 1951-1955,"
    1956.B8
Povey, John F., 1964.B17
Powell, Dilys, 1934.B9
"Power and Conflict in 'The
    Ascent of F.6'," 1964.B13
Precious Five, 1969.A4
Press, John, 1969.B12
Price, The, 1967.B1
Prime (Horae Canonicae 1),
    1951.B12; 1966.A4; 1969.A4;
    1971.B8; 1973.A2; 1974.B18
"Primordial Auden," 1962.B5
"Printing of Auden's Poems
    (1928) and Spender's Nine
    Experiments," 1967.B26
"Problem of Persona in the
    Poetry of W. H. Auden, 1940-
    1966, The," 1967.A1
"Profile of a Poet," 1956.B1
Prologue (The Birth of
    Architecture), 1973.A2
Prologue (O Love, the interest
    itself in thoughtless
    Heaven), 1969.B11
Prologue at Sixty, 1973.A2
Prospero, the Magician Artist:
    Auden's The Sea and the
    Mirror, 1969.A8

137

"Significant Modern Writers: W.
  H. Auden," 1959.B5
Since the External Disorder, and
  Extravagant Lies (Dedica-
  tory to Erika Mann),
  1973.A2
"Sir Lewis Namier and Auden's
  'Musee des Beaux Arts,'"
  1960.B3
Sir, No Man's Enemy, Forgiving
  All (Petition), 1939.B2;
  1965.B28; 1969.A4; 1970.A4;
  1972.A5; 1974.B5
"Sirs, What Must I Do to Be
  Saved?" 1941.B4
"'Situation of Our Time, The':
  Auden in His American Phase,"
  1962.B12; 1964.A4
Sitwell, Edith, 1934.B10;
  1938.B11
"Sixteen Comments on Auden,"
  1937.B2
"Sky Is Aflame, The,"
  1966.B11
Smith, A. J. M., 1935.B6
Smith, Elton Edward, 1970.B21;
  1975.B9
Smith, Janet Adam, 1973.B18
"Snyder, Auden, and the New
  Morality," 1971.B7
So an Age Ended, and Its Last
  Deliverer Died (Sonnets from
  China X) (And an age ended..),
  1966.B19
"Social Philosophy in Auden's
  Early Poetry," 1960.B19
"Some Notes on Auden's Early
  Poetry," 1937.B8
"Some Reasons for Rhyme in
  'Musee des Beaux Arts,'"
  1973.B12
"Some Recent Voices," 1962.B2
"Some Revolutionary Trends in
  English Poetry: 1930-1935,"
  1936.B4
Something Is Bound to Happen
  (The Wanderer) (Chorus)
  (Doom is dark and deeper than
  any sea-dingle), 1948.B1;
  1951.A1; 1972.A5; 1973.A2,
  B9, 1975.B8

Song for St. Cecilia's Day
  (Anthem for St. Cecilia's
  Day), 1967.A3
Song for St. Cecilia's Day: An
  Inaugural Lecture Delivered
  Before the Queen's Univer-
  sity of Belfast on 20th
  November 1967, 1967.A3
Song for the New Year (It's
  farewell to the drawing-
  room's mannerly cry) (Danse
  Macabre), 1939.B2; 1970.A4
Song of the Old Soldier (When
  the sex war ended with the
  slaughter of the grand-
  mothers), 1970.A4
Sonnets from China (In Time of
  War), 1939.B7; 1951.A1;
  1957.B10; 1961.B6; 1965.B23;
  1968.A4; 1969.A9; 1970.A4;
  1971.A2
"Sophistication of W. H. Auden,
  The: A Sketch in Longinian
  Method," 1951.B8
Southworth, James G., 1938.B12;
  1940.B7; 1954.B6
Spain 1937 (Spain), 1937.B15;
  1939.B10; 1940.B4, B6;
  1947.B5; 1959.A1; 1960.B20,
  B24; 1961.B10; 1963.B6;
  1966.B11; 1968.B4, B13, B16;
  1970.A4; 1972.B3; 1973.A1;
  1974.A2
"Spanish Civil War in the
  Literature of the United
  States and Great Britian,
  The," 1960.B13
Sparrow, John, 1934.B11
Spears, Monroe K., 1951.B10,
  B11; 1961.B13; 1962.B15;
  1963.A2; 1964.A4; 1967.B24;
  1968.A5, B12; 1970.B22;
  1974.B18
"Spears on Auden," 1965.B13
Spender, Stephen, 1932.B2;
  1935.B7; 1937.B11; 1938.B13;
  1939.B13; 1946.B5; 1948.B11;
  1949.B11, B13; 1951.B12, B13;
  1953.B4, B5; 1955.B9;
  1970.B23; 1973.B19; 1975.A6

INDEX

INDEX

Though Aware of Our Rank and Alert to Obey Orders (Ode), 1970.A4

"Three English Radical Poets," 1934.B2

"Three Eras of Modern Poetry II," 1938.B11

"Three Who Did Not Make a Revolution," 1952.B8

Through the Looking Glass, 1958.B6; 1973.A2

"Through the Looking Glass," 1944.B4

Thurley, Geoffrey, 1974.B19

Thwaite, Anthony, 1957.B10; 1959.B8; 1974.B20

Toast, A, 1970.A4

Today the Struggle, 1969.B5

"Today the Struggle (A Critical Commentary on Auden's Sonnet-sequence In Time of War)," 1965.B25

"Today the Struggle: A Study of Literature and Politics in England During the Spanish Civil War," 1965.B16

Todd, Ruthven, 1937.B12

Tolley, A. T., 1967.B26; 1968.B14

To My Pupils (Which Side Am I Supposed to Be On) (Ode), 1967.B4; 1968.A3; 1970.A4; 1973.A2

"Tract, A," 1939.B1

Traversi, D.A., 1937.B13

"Trends in Modern Poetic Drama in English, 1900-1938." 1939.B11

Trinculo's Song, 1969.A8

Troy, William, 1937.B14

Truest Poetry Is the Most Feigning, The, 1970.A4

"Truest Poetry is the Most Feigning, The," 1960.B11

T the Great, 1970.A4

Turnell, G. M., 1936.B5

Turpin, Elizabeth R., 1972.B12

"Twelve Poets,: 1934.B12

"Twenty-seven Sonnets," 1939.B7

Twining, Edward S., 1966.A5

"Two Audens, The," 1939.B12

"Two Major Revisions in Auden's 'For the Time Being,'" 1970.B18

"Two Notes on Modern English Poetry: I. Hopkins to W. H. Auden," 1936.B5

"Two Ways of Metaphor," 1962.B17

Two Worlds (The chimneys are smoking, the crocus is out in the border), 1968.A4; 1969.B2

Underneath the Leaves of Life (The Riddle), 1966.A4

"Understanding Auden," 1951.B2

"Understanding Modern Poetry," 1941.B7

Under Which Lyre, 1970.A4

Unknown Citizen, The, 1970.A4

"Untransfigured Scene, The: The Personal Voice in Auden's Early Poetry," 1971.B11

Up There, 1973.A2

Valgemae, Mardi, 1968.B15

"Variant Readings in W. H. Auden's Poetry: Collected Shorter Poems 1927-1957 and Collected Longer Poems," 1970.A6

Venus Will Now Say a Few Words, 1967.B1; 1973.A2

"Verbal Contraption, The: Technique and Style in the Poetry of W. H. Auden," 1969.A6

"Verbal Events," 1974.B9

"Verse Chronicle," 1947.B6

Vespers (Horae Canonicae 5), 1970.A4; 1973.A2

Victor (Victor: A Ballad) (Victor was a little baby), 1962.B7; 1966.B6; 1970.A4, B13

"Virtue and Virtuosity: Notes on W. H. Auden," 1945.B1

Vision and Rhetoric, 1959.B4; 19

Voyage, A, 1971.A2

Voyage, The (I. Whither?) 1973.A2

INDEX

"W. H. Auden as a Critic," 1964.B2

W. H. Auden as a Social Poet, 1973.A1

"W. H. Auden: Aspects of His Poetry and Criticism," 1975.A3

"W. H. Auden at Oxford," 1949.B13

W. H. Auden: A Tribute, 1975.A6

"W. H. Auden: A Tribute," 1974.B8

"W. H. Auden at Swarthmore," 1962.B15

"W. H. Auden: His Characteristic Poetic Mode," 1962.A1

"W. H. Auden in America," 1956.B10; 1964.A4

"W. H. Auden in the 1930's: The Problem of Individual Commitment to Political Action," 1972.B3

"W. H. Auden: 1907-1973," 1974.B15; 1974.B20

"W. H. Auden (1907-1973)," 1973.B19, B20

"W. H. Auden, 1907 to 1973," 1973.B6

"W. H. Auden: Pilgrim's Regress?" 1945.B4

"W. H. Auden: Poet of Anxiety," 1948.B5

"W. H. Auden: Poetry and Journalism," 1958.B1

"W. H. Auden's 'Another Time,'" 1972.B5

"W. H. Auden's 'Autumn Song,'" 1964.B20

"W. H. Auden's Bestiary of the Human," 1966.B1

"W. H. Auden: Select Bibliography," 1965.B22

"W. H. Auden's First Book," 1962.B3

"W. H. Auden's First Published Poems," 1973.B5

"W. H. Auden's 'Meiosis,'" 1970.B15

"W. H. Auden's 'New Year Letter' and Its Relationship to the Rest of His Work," 1968.A3

"W. H. Auden: Spain 1937," 1963.B6

"W. H. Auden's Poetic: A Study of the Relationship Between His Aesthetic Theory and His Theological Point of View," 1963.A1

"W. H. Auden's Supersonnet," 1971.B5

"W. H. Auden's The Shield of Achilles," 1973.B16

"W. H. Auden's 'The Shield of Achilles' and Its Sources," 1974.B5

"W. H. Auden's 'The Shield of Achilles': An Interpretation," 1968.B17

"W. H. Auden: The Farming of a Verse," 1967.B4

"W. H. Auden: The Image as Instance," 1974.B19

"W. H. Auden: The Island and the City," 1969.B11

"W. H. Auden: 'The Most Exciting Living Poet,'" 1952.B1

"W. H. Auden: The Poem as Performance," 1965.B2

"W. H. Auden, The Poet of Angst," 1947.B5

"W. H. Auden: The Poet's Uses of Drama," 1975.A1

"W. H. Auden: The Road from Marx," 1953.B1

"W. H. Auden: The Search for a Public," 1939.B4

"W. H. Auden: The Search for Happiness," 1952.B6

"W. H. Auden, Thirties to Sixties: A Face and a Map," 1969.B2

"W. H. Auden: Two Poems in Sequence," 1961.B9

Wheeler, Charles B., 1966.B19

Wheeler, Edd Dudley, 1971.A4

Wheelwright, Philip, 1962.B17

"When the Pie Was Opened," 1935.B5

When the Sex War Ended with the Slaughter of the Grandmothers (Song of the Old Soldier), 1970.A4

Index